Dedication

This book is dedicated to my daughter Yasmina. Out of all of the people I have encountered in my life, it is your compassion, empathy, and love that bring me to my knees. My life changed for the better when you entered it. You are my guiding light in this world. This book is written for you so that you know where your roots come from. So that you see the strength that runs through your veins.

To my stepmother and biological mother. I was blessed to have you both as strong female figures through different parts of my life. Our souls will meet again someday. To my best friend Vesna who passed away as I was writing this book. Thank you for your unconditional love, your faith in me and your most honest friendship that I will cherish until my flame burns out.

To my father whose unconditional love continues to shine through: the person who has been by me in this life and unconditionally supported me. To my husband Ned, the one person who makes sure that all of my wishes and desires come true, thank you. Thank you for your compassion and patience. Thank you for your support and never-ending love.

To my friends who have been constantly checking on me through my losses. Those that lifted me up when my knees shook and when I had no more strength to move forward. To those that have encountered soul-crushing, debilitating grief, may you find strength through this book to make it through another day. May you draw upon the strength that you possess in you to lead you towards healing.

Acknowledgment

I would like to acknowledge the tremendous amount of effort, persuasion, relentless emotional support, and of course, the editing provided to me very generously by Teresa Miller, RN Case Manager at Idaho Home Health and Hospice. Thank you to Alija, Enida, Denis, Zack, Diana, Antonia and Jelena who have read and re-read many chapters of this book, ensuring that I stayed true to myself as it all began coming together.

Thank you Emina Mustafic for your undying friendship, and for holding me up when fear took over and I began doubting myself. Without their support, guidance, and love it would not have been possible for me to complete this book, for which I am truly thankful to them. I would also like to express my gratitude for the belief instilled by my family and friends that became my guiding light in reliving my darkest moments of grief and despair.

About the Author

Lejla Becirovic is a Bosnian refugee, currently living in the United States and working as a hospice social worker. Having experienced the troubles people face in war, she has dedicated her life to the wider society around her. She now aims to tend towards the needs of others, especially refugees.

As a Social Worker, she is the recipient of two letters from the President of the United States commending her for her outstanding advocacy for disadvantaged populations. She has been nationally recognized as a Hospice Hero in 2018 and 2019 for the exceptional service she provides for her hospice patients.

Lejla fell in love with art at the age of 3 ½ and used her art as an escape during Bosnian's civil war. In 1994 she moved to Twin Falls and quickly fell in love with the area. In 2007 she assisted the 5th-grade class in illustrating a children's book and became co-owner of Rebel Art Studio. She has participated in many local art shows and taught both beginning and intermediate oil painting classes. She was also a featured guest artist at the Full Moon Gallery in

August 2018 and has a collaborative piece that is permanently displayed at Bull Moose Bicycles in Twin Falls. Lejla has donated many paintings to various causes, raising thousands of dollars to help those in need. She has housed numerous homeless women and helped them get on their feet.

Lejla has always been inclined towards art – envisioning and creating it. It's a trait she inherited from her biological mother, but she did not truly divulge in it until encouraged by her step-mother. As a result of their love, dedication, and belief in her, Lejla now shares her masterpieces with the world via the following platforms:

Website: lejla-becirovic.pixels.com
Books website: http://beyondbordersbook.com
Facebook: Art by Lejla
Facebook: Beyond Borders Official Site

Instagram: artbylejla
Instagram for the book: beyondborders

Preface

Certain situations in life contain the power to break a person. To completely cripple their identity. These situations are the ones that we have no control over, no power to change. We are only left to stand and watch the environment around us to be engulfed in flames. The demons wreak havoc; they castrate humanity and lead to the damnation of an individual's soul.

The person is left to bleed, to slowly lose all of their strength and the will to love and live. But only a few outlive the odds. Only a few manage to get through their grief and fill the cracks in their hearts they inherited along this journey of life.

This, here, is my story of how I lost everything dear to me, how I had to leave behind my sanctuary and memories and start anew. My journey of life and all the wisdom it taught me, I now lay open for you to see.

Names have been changed to protect privacy

Contents

Dedication i

Acknowledgment iii

About the Author iv

Preface vi

Introduction 1

Chapter 1 6
I Won't Forget ....

Chapter 2 38
Be Still ....

Chapter 3 93
A Mortal Wound ....

Chapter 4 130
The Color of My Grief ....

Chapter 5 158
In My Purgatory I Found Salvation ....

Chapter 6 195
I Rise ....

Page Left Blank Intentionally

Introduction

My mother always adored the name Lejla. In Arabic, it means *"dusk."* My father boxed in his earlier days, and like any true fan of this sport, he idolized Muhammad Ali whose daughter's name is Layla Ali. A combination of my mother liking this name and my father's infatuation with Muhammad Ali contributed to my getting this name. I was born and raised in Bosnia and Hercegovina. My life has been tainted by trauma and war that I lived with every day of my life. But through trial and turbulence, through moments of despair, I emerged with a life that allowed me to embrace my trauma.

From just a child growing up in the darkest moments of Bosnia to the person I am today, let me narrate my story of how I battled various forms of grief throughout different stages of my life. But just before I let you embark on my journey, let me shed a little light on what inspired me to do so. I graduated with my Masters in Social Work in 2005, and have been in the field of mental health counseling, substance abuse counseling, and hospice throughout my career. As a Hospice Social Worker, I am often overwhelmed to witness numerous people dying or are at the hands of death, battling to make it through the 'today' of their life. In the hospice field, we perceive our work to be a calling than a job. And that it is. To be invited into the final months or days of someone is as sensitive as it is to witness a birth. It leaves all those in this field to be left overwhelmed. Death, that awaits us all, is powerful. It is unique. It is life-changing for those that are to witness it. It is the one thing we as humans are bound to encounter.

Throughout my life, I was urged to combat the distress that occurs within us when we lose a beloved, of not just myself but of those around me as well. The objective is to help those that have encountered hell on earth, lost their loved ones and are lost in their journey of grief, unsure on how to move forward.

"The world breaks everyone, and afterward may we be strong at the broken places."

-Ernest Hemingway

I am writing this book for no other reason but to satisfy the need that has been growing inside me for decades. I have spent 40 years of my life attempting to understand the purpose in life. I am not stepping in front of you as a counselor or a therapist, but as a fellow human being who encountered grief through her journey on this earth. I might not have all the answers when it comes to grief, but I would be cautious of those pretending they do. No one can have the right answer on how to cope with grief. Grief in itself is individualized. Hence, I make no apologies for not having all the answers.

This process is unique for everyone. I learned various things in life, and it took me 40 years to realize that the limit is not the sky, but the universe itself. This book is my testimony. It is my voice that has been wanting to come out since I was born. It is my commitment to growth, and I hope it inspires you, awakens you, and serves you in your journey to healing, growth, and ascension.

After all, I have a contribution to make, and I refuse just to take up space in this world. I believe wholeheartedly that the awakening of our souls will cause us to ascend us beyond hate, beyond ego, beyond turmoil, and beyond grief into a state of greater understanding and acceptance. It will lead us to the awakening of our potential and our ability to transcend beyond shackles of grief. It will lead us to our purpose in this life. It will allow us not only to see our purpose but also to see the purpose of those around us. I am writing this only to show the color of my grief, which is different for everyone. I step out in front of you to bear witness to my shortcomings, my falls, and my rise. Through this book, I will take you through the depths of my hell, my purgatory that haunted me most of my adult life. Some of the things you will discover in this book have been locked away in the deepest pit of my soul.

Some of these events I have pushed away so far, that digging them up has been tormenting and healing at the same time. I have never acknowledged out loud the details of my hell, much less noted it down until now. Walk with me through this book, friend; hold me up should my knees shake. Sit with me in this loneliness and pain of mine, so I am not alone. And if you cry with me, ask yourself if those are my tears in your eyes. How did they get there?

*When I think of death, and of late the idea has come
with alarming frequency,*

*I seem at peace with the idea that a day will dawn when
I will no longer be among those living in this valley of
strange humor,*

*I can accept the idea of my own demise, but I am unable
to accept the death of anyone else,*

*I find it impossible to let a friend or relative go into that
country of no return,*

*Disbelief becomes my close companion, and anger
follows in its wake,*

*I answer the heroic question "Death, where is thy
sting?" with "It is here in my heart and mind and
memories."*

Maya Angelou, When I Think of Death

Chapter 1
I Won't Forget

They say there are no rules in love and war. I learned this to be true early in my life. The effects of war last long after the shooting stops. A war ceases, but its catastrophe remains beyond the expected life span of us mortals. War leaves its imprint in the form of physical and mental ruination. It leaves behind a legacy to enlighten the future generations on the struggles their ancestors did and the many fights they fought relentlessly, just to ensure a better future for us. It is for our sake that our elders fought for freedom, for peace, and for a safe refuge.

A war causes loss that is hard to imagine - loss that devours one's soul. Such a void was left within my soul as well, with even the smallest flicker of hope diminished. It crippled my ability to function, and created grief and loss within me that debilitated and silenced my screams for help. It spread like cancer that devoured me to the core. Such is the state of grief, of the deep agony and despair penetrating our systems, particularly after we lose something or someone that we love. It is the suffering that causes misery in our life. It is the price we pay.

No matter how aware we might be of the truth of losing our dear ones when such a tragedy strikes, we wish to wake up and find it was nothing more than a nightmare. I was also a victim of such nightmares. I was born in the city of Mostar, Bosnia and Herzegovina on February 26th, 1979. My mother went into labor with me at 28 weeks, after her stubborn nature caused her to move a couch by herself so she could vacuum underneath it. It's a nesting period of time that most mothers can relate to. But in my mother's case, moving a couch at 28 weeks of pregnancy was not a smart idea. It initiated a sharp pain in her stomach, a harsh reminder she could not do such things without consequences. And so she went into labor and delivered me two months early.

I was what you call an ELBW *"Extremely low birth weight"* baby, as I came into the world at about 3.7 lbs. My skin and nails were underdeveloped, and I was kept in a makeshift cotton bed. Normal baby blankets irritated my skin and were thus unwelcome. My father reports that my mother kept our home so warm that coming home after a hard day's work was the equivalent of entering a sauna. My nails were not developed and often my parents did not get the typical response from visitors most parents get. *"She is a perfect little angel"* was not something they got to hear too often. Most of the time, the people who came to visit me left without saying a word. The dejection was hurtful for my parents, but it in no way depleted their love towards me. My mother struggled with this. No matter what my looks were like, I was perfect for my mommy. She loved me despite my undeveloped nails. Despite my malnourished little body. Despite my red wrinkly skin. She loved me, even if it bothered her to not hear the typical high pitched excitement of others upon seeing a newborn baby. I was too small, too skinny and more closely resembled a miniature version of an older male than an infant. Conversations with visitors frequently involved prayers for my survival.

They did not expect me to live, but I did, much to everyone's surprise. I guess there was a purpose, a sign that I was meant to do so much more than barely survive. My father tells that when I was born, I was tiny enough to befit his palm conveniently. Both my father and biological mother had no clue what to do with me since the doctors had no hope left of my survival. I am the younger of two children, a hyper-scrawny kid who, for the most part, was very socially awkward and unsure of herself. I owe this trait to the immense lack of belief in my survival. I was always smaller than the average kid my age. As a typical youngest child, I am a bit overly emotional to date, but I have learned to embrace it. This is one of the many traits which makes me who I am, and I would not have it any other way.

When I was 6 months old

When I turned two years old, my mother died of breast cancer at the age of 30. She left my four-year-old brother and me without a mother figure. At that time, I was too young to fully comprehend the gravity of the situation but old enough to crave and mourn my mother's missing presence. I cannot even imagine how hard it must have been for my father, not only to cope with the untimely demise of my mother but also to deal with crying toddlers all by himself. How excruciating it must have been for him when he wiped our tears and put us to sleep, just to shed his own in eerie silence and cold space. My brother was four when our mother died. He retains some memories of her, although even his memories are hard to recall with much detail. In the first grade, he recited a poem about our mother, and by the end of his recital, most of the adults in the room were in tears.

Our town was small, and everyone knew we were the *"orphan kids."* One of my earliest memories with my brother was me trying to beat up some kids because they picked on him in school. How dare they pick on my brother? I would think to myself. Nobody gets to do that. Nobody. All of my life I felt protective of him, even during the times we did not get along.

I could become angry with him easily, but it bothered me when others attempted to talk badly of him. So even though I was the younger sister, I felt a natural urge to stand up to anyone for him. I have no memory of my mother and grew up wondering what she was like. How her forehead would have creased at our mischief or the way her eyes must have lit up at the sight of her beloved children. I wonder how different my life could have been if she was still alive. My father does not talk about his grief or her, even to this date if I ever try to start her topic. He refuses to acknowledge the questions asked about her. So, all the knowledge ⟨...⟩ ral family.

My brother and I with our parents

My father's silence taught me my very first lesson on how to deal with loss. Don't talk about your loss, because if you don't voice it, then in a way it did not happen. A little like the state of being in denial, where you know the tragedy has happened, but you just don't let your brain get familiarized with the sense of it. In fact, I only remember him talking about her a handful of times in my entire life. I cannot imagine how difficult it must have been for him to lose her, considering I am a parent myself today. I cannot imagine the difficulty of having to explain this type of loss to children age four and two years. I believe it was too painful for him to 'remember', and I also believe that he tried very ha

The Orphan Kids

My mother was the second wife of my father. His previous marriage too ended in sorrow, due to a medical condition where their RH factor was incompatible. As a result, both their children were born with a disability and were unable to cope with life. One of their children died due to SIDS, while the other suffered from a genetic disorder and passed away at the age of two. My half brother and sister, Jasmin and Jasmina, today rest in their eternal cribs at Ljubuski's cemetery. The iron baby cribs were handcrafted by my father, his last act of love and devotion to his first children.

Those iron cribs have withstood years of harsh weather and cruel war that hit my country in the 1990s. The two cribs that will forever cradle these two sleeping angels. The death of their children took a drastic toll on the marriage, and soon they found unable to cope with each other. They say two broken people can either complement one another or break each other beyond repair. My father and his first wife were unable to move past two dead children and eventually split for the sake of themselves. My father divorced his first wife, and after that, as fate decreed it, he met my biological mother.

My sister Jasmina's Grave

My father made sure to keep my mother's clothes and journals in a small storage unit under our yellow couch back in our apartment in Bosnia. As a child, it was a treasure box for me. Mother's clothes were neatly folded and stored, along with the jewelry she would wear to accentuate her clothing with, broaches included. There were also paintings and journals. As a child, I would pull her clothes and journals out, stare at them, and wonder who she was. She was a mystery to me. All that I knew of my mother, came from her belongings that had burnt to ashes when we had to flee a war-stricken Bosnia.

The remainder of my knowledge regarding my mother comes from the random stories narrated by various family members. My own mother was also depicted and painted for me to visualize through the good wordings of others. I let my imagination work the charms of having a vivid image of her painted in my memory - a place where she is etched till date. They say she was a woman who was born outside of her time. An old soul that turned everything she touched into gold. She was a self-taught artist, designer, and an amazing

My mother wearing the clothes she designed herself

My maternal family narrated the inner turmoil she faced when she was diagnosed with cancer. Back then, the norm in Bosnia was that the family of the patient hid their illness from them. Hence, she was showered with the undeterred hope that instilled belief into her that everything would turn out to be fine. But when she was left alone, in the doctor's room, with a file of hers on the desk, she could not help herself and began reading the contents to discover the truth.

The illness was devouring her on a daily basis, leaving the once strong woman weak. When combating cancer, her sole concern was the well-being of her two children. The worry was so intense that she expressed it even in the last words she tried so hard to voice out to her sisters, but failed. But my aunts are sure she was trying to tell them to *"Watch out for my kids."*

My mothe... passed away on o... uski

My mother's grave

How could my father not be devastated? My mother's death left behind destruction that still echoes in my life. She left behind abandonment and confusion that is hard to explain. She left behind two children and a husband who loved her dearly. With each passing day, her presence became more daunting to my father, with no source of redemption. His grief over losing his friend, lover, and the mother of his children became too much for him to bear. Hence, with time, he felt in our best interest was to get remarried.

Desperation led my father to make a wonderful decision when he sought help to raise his children. He brought home with him a lady with a pleasant aura. When I asked this person if she was to be my new mommy, my stepmother said that she simply could not say no, and this became the sole reason she decided to marry my father. I sat on her lap and asked her this question. I must have been about three years old at that time, but I clearly understood what was going on. She said that her decision of marrying my father was not for him, not for love, not for a sense of security, and not for support, but for us. She said she simply could not say *no* and joined the family shortly. Her reasons sufficed in speaking for her as a person.

My father married a woman who was wonderful to us and did her best to ensure we were safe and taken care of in the best manner possible. She was nowhere near that dreadful stereotype of a stepmother who, once she marries your father, unveils herself to be a tyrannical woman, tormenting the children and treating them like slaves. No, our stepmother was an angel in disguise, a form of compensation from God for calling my mother back when her children were mere toddlers.

She accepted my brother and me for who we were, like her own, and spoiled us just like how our biological mother would have. She did all that she could to never let us have a moment of resentment or bitterness toward her. And I don't think my brother and I ever could. She made my life better and made me see my potential as an individual.

My stepmother was a wonderful woman who loved us with all of her heart. But this is not a story of an orphan. This is not a story of victims. It is a story of love, loss, exploration, growth, connection, and ascension. This is a story of the desire to live, to have a better tomorrow than yesterday, and to elevate the spirits of oneself and the others around us.

One thing that I have in common with my biological mother is my love of art - a priceless inheritance, and one of her attributes to me that I perceive to be her last gift. As long as I can remember, I have painted. I loved Michelangelo so much that as a child I would dream that one day with hard work I would be as good as him. At an age when other kids play outdoors with one another, chasing each other or partaking in sports, I preferred to stay home and paint to my heart's desire.

Rather than disregarding my passion and labeling it a waste of time, my stepmother and father would encourage this, and bestow me with a myriad of paints and brushes on my birthdays. There was a mesmerizing enchanted spell I associated with the motion of mixing colors and letting the tip of the brush tarnish the white, only to reveal a whole new spectrum of colors onto it.

When we escaped Bosnia, all of our belongings were left behind to pay the price of the calamity that struck the entire country. All of my paintings burned up. When the canvas was set ablaze, so was my desire to paint. My passion and love were caught up in the fiery red flames of an inextinguishable fire, leaving behind ashes.

Miraculously, my desire to paint was resurrected only a few years ago. I suddenly felt my connection with my first ever love reignite ferociously. I felt an urge pull me toward my brushes, and I lifted them up. The smooth and grainy texture nudged me into seeking pleasure from painting once more. When I twisted the cap off my paints, their smell lingered in the empty space, pushing my senses to savor the experience. That was the exact moment when I lost myself. The world around me was no longer in existence, and my vision could only take in the purity of the canvas. For me, there is nothing more satisfying than the moment I lose track of time while painting.

Today, I paint to calm my nerves, to process my grief, and to express things I hold inside me when I cannot find words. I extend my emotions to flow freely onto the canvas and let them reveal themselves. If someone is to watch me paint, they would see I am in a trance, for painting truly captivates me, lulling me into losing myself in its embrace. It is my greatest pleasure, and my means to let my woes out.

But why do I need to have such a means of expression?

Well, I grew up in a culture of body shaming, school shootings, illness, political bullies, hate, war, and destruction. I lived in a world that was based on unachievable goals and political enslavement - a world scorching with pride, prejudice, loathing, and hostility. This enslavement exists even today as I am a college graduate enslaved by never-ending student loans - a first-generation refugee trying to make something of my life and secure safe passage.

I grew up in a culture where the healthcare system promotes illness over cure, where nutrition is portrayed as a poison, where the justice system diminishes the meaning of justice as it extends protection to criminals, where the government continues to enslave us with biased policies under the pretext of betterment. Our best friends create abandonment, and our loyalty betrays those closest to us, making us question ourselves and why we ever relied on someone else. I grew up in a world where hate is a learned and readily adopted social trait, and greed is a norm. It's a world where modesty, virtues, morals, and ethics are challenged with uncertainty. I live in a world of virtual reality, where people are disconnected from their humanity and connected to a pretentious manner.

We focus on portraying perfection on social media, blurring our flaws just to comply with the ignorant beauty standards. A virtual world where the lights are readjusted and the focus is on the outer beauty, fogging the surroundings - a notion that encourages to acknowledge only physical beauty, overlooking other possibilities. It's where selfies are more important than the beauty of one's soul. This virtual world has been created to distract us from the progression of our humanity. This is the virtual world where we are coerced into creating virtual cemeteries, virtual condolences, and virtual support, forgetting all about the physical world.

I am just another soul brave to walk this earth and immerse herself in this human experience. I am imperfect in every sense of the word. It is those imperfections that have been perfect for me. It is those imperfections that have taken me right here to this spot. I am a person with a desire to be accepted and loved. I aspire to be a better version of myself every time I take a glimpse of my reflection. I wish to be a role model for my progeny and to let the fire of gratitude prolong. I am you.

***

I was born and raised in Bosnia and Hercegovina, which during the civil war in the 1990s, gained independence from former Yugoslavia. I come from a small country located in the center of Europe which, throughout the years, has witnessed more wars than one is willing to admit. Bosnia and Hercegovina is a small country in South Eastern Europe on the Balkan Peninsula, named after the Balkan Mountains that stretch proudly through Bulgaria to the Black Sea.

Not only is Bosnia famous for its breathtaking sceneries, but also for its scarring war history. Its history dates back to settlements in the Neolithic Age about 12,000 years ago. This land has seen ages of love and loss year after year on end. Ages of wars have soaked its soil in blood. From the Roman Empire to the Ottoman Empire, and all of the others since then, have shaped this country's architecture that stands even today.

From dismantling to reconstruction, the people adopted numerous heritage and cultures of all its settlers and conquerors. It is by far one of the most beautiful countries in the world. Stepping on its soil feels as if you are stepping back in time. Various castles still stand as tombstones to kings who ruled over the land. The majestic stacking of bricks, stones, and boulders of ruination captivates the tourists to the point of being lost in awe. Former Yugoslavia was the hubcap of forces that fought Nazis persistently during World War II. Under the direction of its leader, Tito, this country flourished to new beginnings. After his death, each state within Yugoslavia began separating into independent states. But the hope that came with a new sunrise for a new tomorrow turned out to be rather short-lived, much to the dismay of the locals. A land in which Bosnians, Croats, and Serbs had lived as brothers and sisters for centuries was now unraveling to appalling displays of hatred. The once peaceful and united community now expressed bitterness for the other, wanting nothing more than bloodshed and separation.

Bosnia declared independence on April 5th, 1992. I believe that one of the reasons Serbia did not want separation of the states was for fear of not having access to the Adriatic Sea. The Adriatic Sea falls amongst one of the most popular tourist spots in Central Europe for its alluring blue opacity, but its expanse has more value than its beauty. But there are many other reasons this war happened. The collapse of the Soviet Union had a lot to do with many wars in Europe, not just the war in Bosnia. Greed and hatred were reasons for this war, as was betrayal, and the ability to hate each other is the reason for this war. And the effect of the war? Ethnic cleansing and crimes against humanity, as well as the desire to erase us and the history of our existence from the face of this earth, was the effect of this war. Bosnia rose out of the ashes of Yugoslavia after its declaration of independence. Serbia and Croatia initially wanted Bosnian territory, and to cleanse their land of Bosniaks. These Bosniaks are a beautiful mixture of Muslims, Christians and Orthodox people who have lived on this land for centuries. Croatia wanted a piece of the pie and attacked Bosnia and Hercegovina from the south. Serbia attacked from the north.

Bosnia had to defend itself even though it had nowhere near enough ammunition to do so. One attack led to another and before the nations knew it, each state began separating from Yugoslavia, initiating war. This was not the end to the monstrosity. With the war came ethnic cleansing. The locals' bloodlust was unwilling to stop at just capturing land. They wanted to be able to spread their religion everywhere. Anyone not sharing the same belief was to be wiped off. 104,732 people were slaughtered like cattle. The human race was no longer of value. Massacres turned into a norm, and the land was conquered with all-consuming greed. Women and men were separated into concentration camps. Whole families were executed at gunpoint. People were beheaded and their heads were used as soccer balls. Men, women, children and the elderly, the able-bodied and the disabled, were sodomized. Women of all ages were raped while the men in their family were forced to watch. People were set on fire. Snipers killed people and their corpses decomposed in the streets for days before it was safe enough for families to retrieve the corpse and provide them with a burial. Killing someone was simply not good enough, so their bodies were dismembered to ensure that proper burial could not be done.

Greed is a state of mind that spreads like a poison within mankind, causing hallucinations that trick the mind into wanting more than what is requisite. Greed deludes us into believing that we always have insufficient materials at our disposal, that we should acquire more than we can handle. Mercy was considered an act of weakness, not granted to even the young, the senior, the female, and those with a disability. The majority of the victims were Bosnians. The Serbs dug the once solid ground into mass graves and mercilessly filled them with corpses. Some of these graves are still being uncovered.

People are still looking for the remains of their loved ones to provide them with a burial, as many are still missing. Serbs slaughtered around 8,000 people in the town of Srebrenica in one day. This war is known as the bloodiest war since the Holocaust. But this is not the first time that this land went through a war. I guess humanity fails to reconcile with its past mistakes, or maybe they get addicted to repeating the same calamity. Apart from the large-scale tragedy that was inflicted on the people, the war also played host to a personal tragedy – a story narrated by my beloved grandmother.

My grandmother told me that she was captured by the Germans during World War II. I spent quite a bit of time living with her in her little condo, where I would keep her company. This condo was located in the middle of Ljubuski, a small ancient town formed in the early 1400s in the southern part of Hercegovina. As I recall this, I still smell the aroma of bean soup vividly. It was one of my favorite traditional meals, one which only my grandmother could make the way I liked. I must have been about eight when she told me about my grandfather, a man I never met as he had passed away even before I was born.

I can close my eyes and see her deep set of wrinkles adorning her face like river beds. They curved whichever way they wanted to on her face. She always kept her white hair short and styled in a perm that framed her face. Thick glasses made her eyes look bigger. Her eyes were like two hard jewels that would light up at any opportunity to teach. A set of eyes that had seen peace overturning by years of war, murder, and destruction, all that came with World War II. She had a smile that would pull you deep into the depth of her kind soul. From the undertows of her smile, one could clearly see the emotions she suppressed.

These emotions were a part of her existence now, and she chose to keep them tucked at bay, as they had the ability to welcome tears. When she smiled, the corners of her mouth would curl upward, revealing her pearly white teeth. My grandmother was a proud woman who endured endless beatings from the years of a hard life. But she stood strong. She was an epitome of wonder, and all those who knew her would be lost in her trance, thinking about how a woman who aged witnessing bloodshed could still stand strong. The answer to this lied in the resilience she possessed. Each story was a lesson ensuring I know where I come from.

"Don't ever forget what blood runs through your veins. Don't ever forget where you come from." The sound of her voice still echoes in my ears.

"I won't grandma, I won't." My typical reply to assure her that I would obey.

My grandmother would explain that during World War II, my family was the hubcap of an underground mission that sent food and medicine to the Yugoslavian army fighting against the Germans. She was captured on several occasions by the Germans for smuggling and helping the Yugoslavian army. But she stood strong for what she believed in. Even in the face of death, she stood strong when most in her place would prove to be cowardly. She was not amongst the ones to betray their motherland. When captured by the Germans, she requested that they allow her to put on her best suit before being led to the field where she would be executed.

I wondered out loud what fear one must encounter in a situation like this. *"Were you scared, grandma?"*

But she was willing to die for what she believed in. This was how determined she was for this war. Subsequently, this made me question what I was willing to die for. A vague question, but its answer runs deeper than I could have imagined.

"I was scared," she replied, *"which person isn't? But I never let them see this."*

My grandmother was a proud woman, who carved her own path for death. Even if she were fated to die that day at the hands of the Germans, she would not have let them find pleasure in executing her. She was willing to die an honorable death of a soldier. Fate is a strange thing. She was not meant to die and through strings pulled by connections with a family friend, the monastery in Ljubuski, she escaped by the skin of her teeth. Not once but twice.

On the other hand, my grandfather was shackled and placed in a barn where he was detained for some time. My grandmother told me that his hands were wrapped in chains, which were attached to a huge nail in the wall. It took him several days to work that nail out. Pulling, tugging, and allowing the nail to slowly begin grinding the stone it was pounded in. When his hands were tired, he also used his teeth. In the meantime, he suffered through regular beatings at the hands of Nazis attempting to get the names of the others who had helped smuggle medicine and food to the Yugoslavian army. Once freeing himself, my grandfather patiently waited for a German soldier to come in and give him another one of those beatings. The soldier came in, but to his surprise, he found my grandfather free and the fight began. He killed this solder as quickly as he could, dressed in his clothing, and escaped the German camp. My grandmother said he practically walked out of camp and escaped. The proof of his courage was the glowing red marks as a result of the chains, which he wore proudly. They were his battle scars and they reminded him of the torture encompassing Bosnia.

My grandfather was no less of a warrior and perhaps that is why he was in love with my grandmother. My family was amongst the hubcap fighting against the Germans, in the hopes of freeing our land from the vile invaders. The country was ruined, and the German army left no stone unturned when it came to destroying our state. The majority of people were against the Germans, but a minority aided them. And so, as a result of a few traitors hiding amongst the rebels, my grandfather's two brothers were killed by their neighbor. The neighbor was working for the Germans and somehow became aware of my family supplying the local army with food and medication in secrecy.

My father was a child when his two uncles were shot. One of them was hit with the barrel of the gun, and his corpse was thrown into the river, while the other was shot behind the grain mill in Bascina (a resort place a short drive from Ljubuski), during World War II. The neighbor was later arrested by our defending army, and as a precautionary measure, the defending army was about to arrest his children as well. My grandfather stepped in and protected this man's children from the defending army, as he believed they were innocent. The children intended no harm and had no motive or hand in their father's betrayal either.

He did all in his best to protect the children of the man who had brutally murdered his brothers, believing the children were clean of the poor choices their father made.I remember the little stories my grandmother narrated to me, to cherish and forever uphold the struggle they went through. She also told me these stories in the hopes of prolonging the history of our ancestors and passing it down to the progeny so that they too would grow up respecting their heritage. But a tragedy took place. Long after the war was over, my grandfather was grief-stricken to the extent that he resorted to alcohol just to be able to cope with the nightmares that followed ever since. The torture inflicted on him as a POW back in the German prison caused horrendous trauma within him. Eventually, he died of alcohol poisoning. I never got a chance to meet him, his brave actions are enough to cause my heart to swell with pride, and fill me with gratitude toward him

My grandfather's grave

It gives me chills to remember this story. But it's the story of my grandmother's and grandfather's life, and this book helps me write down their story. This story is a reminder of where I come from and what kind of strength runs through my veins.

"I won't forget grandma, I won't forget."

***

The heat of Hercegovina summers can be excruciating. My favorite spot in Bascina, a resort place just outside of Ljubuski where we owned land and ancestral home, was sitting on a large rock in the thick shadow of an oak tree. This shadow provided me with some much-needed refuge. I must have been about 7 years old. My cousin and two wicked girls had been throwing rocks at me. I remember being heartbroken over my cousin not standing up for me. What hurt the most is that he was the one that threw the rocks at me too. This incident had not been witnessed by any adults, and it would have been useless to try to tell on him.

So the best thing I could do was to sit under this ancient oak tree and cry with some privacy. A gentle breeze would help dry my tears, so if someone was to see me they would not even notice that I was crying. This was the first time in my life I felt the betrayal of someone close to me. Wasn't it my cousin's role to protect me? Was this what it felt to die at the hands of your trusted ones? This was it.

Although this is one of the first memories of my life, and my cousin and I were just kids who would naturally fight as children do, I could not help but join the dots. The fact was that this type of betrayal was what our war felt like, except on a much larger scale. This was what Bosnians went through when some of us turned traitorous, back-stabbing whom we once deemed to be our brothers and sisters. And for whom? We failed to value the blood of our own kind and then we wonder why we are not at peace.

***

Once again, we Bosnians found ourselves in war. Did we not learn much from the past? What were we fighting for? This war was blamed on religion, much like most wars are. The truth is that all wars happen, and they use this same excuse, but underneath it all, is greed, power, and money. When will it be enough? There have been so many wars through history, yet we forget that it's mostly the innocent who die. And for what? At what cost? For other people's agendas? The innocent are merely pawns in this game of chess. Politicians start wars and the sheep follow. Nobody wins, except for those who are in power as always.

Bosnia began getting hits from the north from the heavily armed Serbia, which was performing ethnic cleansing on people. From the south, Croats were beginning to arrest us and throw us into concentration camps. We bled as the world watched us fall apart bit by bit. They broke us from within. Once they had hollowed us they started to take hits at our walls. This was my history, filled with sorrow, stress, trauma, tragedy, and horror, but most of all resilience and a will to overcome all negativity. After all, life is all about moving on and going with the flow. To adapt to what is thrown at you, as you lock the memories of your dearly departed in your heart and soul forever.

"Grief is like the ocean; it comes in waves, ebbing and flowing. Sometimes the water is calm, and sometimes it is overwhelming. All we can do is learn to swim."

Vicky Harrison

Chapter 2
Be Still

My grandmother lived through World War II, when the political situation got increasingly worse. She was the first one to express her concern over the outcome of the war in the early 1990s. While people talked about the separation of Yugoslavia - about it being made into a separate state - my grandmother's knowledge and wisdom led us to conclude we had to flee our motherland in the hopes of securing safety.

Back in Bosnia, we lived in a small condo on the 4th floor in our building. This was my home, where I loved indulging in the arts. My biological mother was an artist, too, and I inherited this trait of hers. I felt that art was not just my passion, but brought me closer to her as well. As a child, whenever I drew, I would lose track of my surroundings and time. I would only cease to exist at the moment next to the piece I was working on.

I felt differently when we had people come over to our house before the war. My parents made me pull out my art to show it off in front of them. But I did not want to do that.

I wanted to preserve my art for my eyes only. I preferred staying home most of the time, as I felt much closer to my biological mom that way - being near to where her things were kept. For most of my days, I would prefer to draw than go out and play with kids my age. I felt more grown up than the other children my age. They would be kicking the ball around or playing in the open under the vast blue sky, whereas I couldn't care less about it. I would stay in the comforts of my apartment, where all I wanted was for my paintings to be just mine than to be shown to others. I knew my father and step-mother were excited to show off my art, but I preferred to keep it private - just to myself.

To everyone else, my paintings were meant to be glorified and exhibited for compliments, but they meant much more than that to me. I never said this out loud, as the reason was meant to be known only by my heart. But today, I share this with all of you. Whenever I painted or sketched, I channeled my feelings onto the canvas before me. It was my way of expressing all that I felt and all that I saw, rather than to communicate verbally about my feelings. I was not good with words or communicating in general, so painting became my means of comfort.

As soon as my brush would hit the paper, all the sentiments within me would pour out onto the blank paper, until the swirls and drops of paint eternally displayed all the locked up thoughts in my mind. Once I was done, there would lie before me a free depiction of the fragments of my imaginations, desires, and notion.

Back in school, I had good grades and scored mostly A's - except in English Language. My English teacher was a lady who had recently moved to Bosnia from England. However, she was the meanest and most awful teacher I ever had - unlike the rest of my teachers. Despite getting straight A's in other subjects, I failed her class and was the least bothered to bother with acquiring this language - all due to her rude behavior.

Back then, I didn't think I would ever need to use English, but when I moved to the US, I thought about my teacher a lot and how I should have been more attentive in her class. Perhaps things could have been more comfortable in the beginning then if I had been equipped with the basics of the English language. Back in school, my focus was on the arts. It was my favorite subject, hands down. And the best memory that I have was of my art teacher who was a nurturing soul.

He saw the talent in me and encouraged me to continue doing more of arts. The more someone encouraged me to pursue my passion, the more I was fascinated and driven to continue excelling in arts. I grew up with Maria, and we would see each other every weekend. Her grandmother was neighbors with my grandmother. She used to make me catch up with her, and she would bring her Barbie dolls for us to play with every time I visited my grandmother. She was my best friend in Bosnia, despite us not sharing the same classes.

She was a quiet, reserved and calm girl, just like me. Her personality was what attracted me to be with her, and that is what I needed - someone as laid back and calm like myself. I was an introvert, to put it simply, and not fond of social gatherings. Hence, I needed to befriend someone with a similar nature to mine.

I was also hesitant to mingle with the other children my age, as I used to think more than a typical child. I would analyze the most trivial of things at a very young age, which would make me very emotional. Maria was the only one who was the least fazed by my zoning out. The war started when people started to vote for a separate state. When the first people settled in Bosnia, they enriched the land with history and culture.

But all of that was lost under the dark shadow of greed sprawling all over the land. The main spark that ignited the war was religion, but as a kid, I was never bothered by my friends' religion, nor were they by mine. When I came to the US at the age of 14, we had been in the midst of the war for 4 years, but Maria did not. She and her family did not face the need to leave the southern part of Hercegovina, as she was Christian.

During those times, it was mandatory for everyone to be a Christian in the southern part of the country. It did not matter if we were practicing or not - as long as our religion was Islam, we were the ones being forced to vacate our motherland. The Christians got to keep their belongings and households, while ours were brutally plucked out from the roots to swipe the entire ethnic population. It was ethnic cleansing - there's no question about it.

As I said before, Bosnia and Hercegovina was the center of old Yugoslavia, with a beautiful mix of Muslims, Croats and Orthodox Christians. There were not many Muslims in the southern part of Bosnia, as most occupied the northern part. But Muslims, Croats and Orthodox people all experienced war and were affected by it, depending on which part of Bosnia and Hercegovina they lived in. Back then, Croatia wanted to take over part of southern Bosnia and Hercegovina, and so did Serbia, which wanted to occupy the northern part. All the people living in the region were affected, yet Muslims were the biggest casualty. Our war started with Serbia initially attacking Slovenia, but that was short-lived and ended very quickly. Then Croatia attacked Bosnia, and that did not last very long either. Finally, Croatia and Bosnia joined in to fight off Serbia. A world where it seemed everyone was attacking everyone else.

But in any hell, angels rise. There were good people on all sides. There were bad people as well. Encyclopedias could be written about our wars attempting to explain why they happened. Most of us did not want war. We accomplished nothing. Politicians, though, stirred the pot and created hatred. They intended for a mass massacre of all the Muslims in Bosnia and Hercegovina before they could invade the land.

Looking back now, I find it hard to remember life before the war. My mind has been blocked by the trauma I suffered through and after the war. The effects of such incidents and traumas irreversibly impact you. New memories flood in and overshadow the old ones. Our mind no longer allows us to connect back with what once was the worst nightmare any human can ever think of, which leaves your heartbeat frantic and your forehead a pool of sweat. When we escaped Bosnia, all of my belongings were left behind and burnt to ashes, including the memoirs of my biological mother and all of the paintings. In hindsight, a part of me was left behind, and I was never in touch with the inner artist until a couple of years back. After that horrid past, I could not muster up the courage to paint once again, and I had forgotten what it felt like to feel the touch of a paintbrush under my fingertips.

Back in our condo, our TV in the living room was always turned on the news station. We would watch, eyes glued to the screen as our politicians decided our fate. War was brewing, that much was for certain. The night before this hell was unleashed on us, I watched Milosevic talk on TV, about cleansing the land of our people. What an angry man! I thought to myself. His chubby red face with its little nose and jaws made him look like a Pitbull, almost salivating at the hate he was spewing. His looks made me laugh out loud. I was already in my pajamas and my stepmother hurried towards the TV to shut it off.

"*It is past your bedtime*," she said, as she motioned for me to go to bed. I crawled in and she tucked me in for what it would be the last time we would exist in some sort of normalcy. I lay in bed, hearing the noises of my stepmother making in the kitchen, washing the dishes from our dinner. We ate baked potatoes and chicken that night. I loved this dish, especially the potatoes that would stick to the sides of the pan and make a crisp sound in my mouth when I ate them.

Those were my favorite, and my stepmother would pile them up on my plate each time she would prepare this dish. Now I lay in bed, staring at the ceiling and thinking about the cleansing Milosevic had talked about. What did that mean? What kind of cleansing was he talking about? I don't remember falling asleep that night, but I know it was late by the time I eventually nodded off.

The day started with dread. I was sleeping soundly in my bed, only to be awoken by emergency sirens going off. A roar of emergency sirens echoed overhead, wailing and ripping through the silence that had preceded it in the once peaceful city of Ljubuski. A southern little town in Bosnia and Hercegovina, violence was a distant concept here.

We lived on the 4th floor of our building. It was a simple condo that housed all of my childhood memories. It was where my biological mother's clothes and journals were stored. In the early hours, before the sun came up, muffled sounds of panic echoed in the hallways of the building. Panic-stricken people began running down the stairs towards the basement, like a stampede of buffalo herds.

We could not quite figure out what was happening, but we knew we needed to join our neighbors in the basement of the building. Later, we found out it was due to the *"enemy"* planes bombing our town when we had least expected it. Ten-year-old me in panic and fear had put her jeans on inside out as I could not see well to get dressed in the dark. But I had no choice - it was either that or let my fear take over and immobilize me. My hands and body shook as I put one pant leg on and then the other, and all the while the sound of the sirens resonated within my body.

My family and I ran down the stairs as fast as we could.

However, even though I had run down the same landing of stairs a thousand times before, this felt different from rushing to go outside and play. This time, we were running to save our lives. I held on to the railing tightly this time, careful to not fall, for fear of my shaky legs giving out underneath me. The air smelled different. The stench of fear spread throughout the hallways. None of us knew what was bound for us, but we all shared the same destination in mind – shelter. The basement was darker than usual. A small candle on a makeshift table illuminated a cardboard box with the word *"Rice"* on it. All of my neighbors were huddled together around it - some crying, some as silent as the air before a massive tornado hits. The entire basement was engulfed in a vacuum. Those crying let out silent sobs to prevent the enemies from gathering our whereabouts. The ten-year-old me, not quite a child and not quite a woman, stood there wobbly with awkwardness and lack of confidence in the basement, hoping nobody would notice that my jeans were inside out.

I backed into a corner, ensuring that I wouldn't be seen. If the adults were unable to comprehend the situation's potential, then how could I have? All I knew was to blindly follow my family and hope no one of us would be a victim to what was about to hit us. I shifted my focus to the fabric of the pant pockets sticking out like wings on my bottom. The thought made me chuckle. If only they were wings, surely I would have flown away from this place - far away to a land of a sanctuary.

The flickering flame of a candle lit up a portion of the basement only to show fear on people's faces. Dark circles around almond-shaped eyes, chests pulsating from the tears that were about to release - much as water comes out of a wellspring – these were the features of this barren land. There was nowhere to run. We were stranded like a father outside the room waiting for his unborn child. Only, we were living in undeniable fear.

Do you know what that feels like to a child? To tremble in fear with nowhere to run? To be abruptly woken up from a peaceful slumber, only to dive into a war with no options. The uncertainty hovered above us like thick clouds, thick enough to be sliced through with a knife. And then the sirens stopped. Silence filled the air all throughout Ljubuski. We all exchanged glances brimming with horror. Everyone was afraid even to heave a sigh as our collective heartbeat slowed down its pace. A man spoke in the basement. "*This is the calm before the storm.*"

"What storm is going to hit us?" I thought to myself. The thought of this made my fear grow. *What will happen to us?*

I was not ready to die or lose my family. What did death feel like? In my 10 years on this earth, I had never given death much thought, except for the time my grandmother told me about her experience of being lead to the execution field by German soldiers. I guess children are not supposed to give death much thought.

The condo on the top-one side was ours - parts of it look burnt-up. We don't know who lives there now

Yet, a child in war faces a life that differs from an idyllic childhood. Being attacked for no reason has the effect of diminishing a child's innocence if they are a citizen of a war-torn country. Your childhood gets snatched right before your eyes, and all you can do is to take it all in with quivering lips, spending each second wondering what wrong you did to be punished this way. A child in war watches their parents, siblings, relatives, and friends be murdered right before their eyes, and fear leaves them rooted to their spot. What else can a child do anyways, except shed tears in silence and tremble endlessly? But why should we worry our mind as long as we get to sleep safe and sound in our bed every night? Humanity, in general, encompasses the most selfish form of existence. As long as we are safe from the horrors of this world, we only express our empathy towards those suffering. We possess the power to help someone out of their misery but don't. This is what I experienced firsthand during the bloodiest war in Europe after the Holocaust.

Back in the basement, I thought of death. I thought about it a lot. *"I don't want to die, not like this,"* I thought to myself, *"Not like this and not today."* What would it be like to be crushed by the building? Buried alive by its debris. *"I am not ready to die,"* I thought again. Just as that image came into my mind, the sound of detonations ripped apart the silence like a child ripped from its mother's arms.

One after another, explosions filled the air. Each explosion made us flinch, *"Will this building cave in on us?"*

We spent that day in the basement huddled together, all of our neighbors and us. We counted each breath we took and familiarized ourselves with each others' faces of despair until we knew each and every crease. We had all the time in the world to anticipate the next explosion, yet each second also hinted that perhaps we were next to die. Our pounding hearts drummed wildly in our chest. I can still vividly hear the wild thumps of my frantic heartbeat. I told myself just to be still. I believed that if I were adequately still, we would be safe. I deluded myself into thinking that our existence would be spared. Confused and dazed, we listened to explosions outside damning the city, wondering if our building would come caving in on us next. Wondering if we will survive and if this horror will cease. Wondering who did not survive and which building exploded. *Did someone I know die?*

There was a strange feeling of relief hearing bombs destroy a part of town that was further from us. Relief! This was one of the effects of war. The once caring neighbors turned onto each other. The brothers and sisters who once would have sacrificed themselves for each other now hoped the other died and they got to live one more day - even if they would have died next themselves.

War turned everyone selfish. The conflicting feeling of relief that we are not dying, even if it was devastating someone else's life, leaves you feeling bitter for the rest of your life. It is devastating not knowing if it was one of our friends or family who had just died. A quick celebration to be alive shattered with the thought: *will we survive?* But I did not survive - at least, not the 10-year-old me. War kills the innocence of children. It kills hopes and dreams. It killed eleven members of my family. The magic and mystery of life you experience as a child dies in the war. Instead of growing up believing in Santa during Christmas time, these children are made to see the harsh reality of this life and war, and all the havoc it wrecked on a once pleasant town and family.

My brother and father escaped at the beginning of this. This hell started with men of all ages getting picked up by the police and taken to camps. My aunt was quick to have my father transported in the middle of summertime. It was a typical Hercegovina's summer, the kind where the sun heats the stone so much that you can feel the heat radiate even in the evening time, until the wee hours of the morning. He laid down in the back of her car and she covered him with heavy blankets, stocking them to the top of the car so that even if we got stopped at the border, they would have to remove a whole bunch of them before they would find him.

Even though my father won't talk about this, what I do know is that when they reached Croatia, they were stopped by the police at the border. He could hear them question my aunt as to what she was transporting. Each question they asked made his pulse stutter, thinking this was the moment they would be caught and killed, or taken back to the concentration camp before being tortured to their death.

She planned to run the car should the police ask her to step out, risking death. This would have been more merciful a fate than getting caught and tortured. But with luck, she was not asked to get out of the car and was waved to pass through. Once inside a safe zone, she pulled all the blankets off of him and found him passed out from all of the heat. Yet, the sight of her brother passed out was not the least bit worrying to my aunt. She heaved a sigh of relief, having rescued her brother to safety.

My father does not speak of where he was for a period of one year after this. Maybe his mind blocked out that particular time of his life, or maybe it took him immense courage to shun the nightmares to the deepest pit within him. We were not told where my father was at all, since it was feared someone could have coaxed the truth from us children. I cannot imagine what it was like for him to be separated from his children. He must have spent his time worrying about our life and praying for us - as we did for him. I craved for the embrace of my father and brother. Even if my brother and I did not get along well, I knew I wanted for him to live and to be able to join us one day.

I stayed with my grandmother, who lived a few blocks from the bus station. In June of 1992, screaming and wailing sounded from the bus station a few blocks from my grandmother's home, bringing tears to our eyes. All the men were initially invited to come to the police department, to sign up their families as well as to sign up men to join in the army. It was a lie. This was the easiest way for police to gather all the Muslim men and make their jobs easier. A line of men waited in front of the police station to sign up, only to be arrested and taken to the bus station and then transported to concentration camps.

Families were separated at the bus stop. Wives fell down to their knees to beg for the life of their loved ones. Boys and men of all ages, infants and elderly alike, were mercilessly ripped from mothers' and wives' arms. The dread in the air gave away the fact that our world was about to be turned upside down. While it was a relief and blessing that my brother and father escaped the clutches of death, my heart, even as a child, clenched at the sight of the cruelty before me. Busses rolled through the town. The faces of confused souls stared out the windows, hoping someone would come to their rescue. It was as if they were cattle that were being taken to slaughter. And most of them met that horrible fate. Concentration camps were unsurprisingly awful. Some of the schools were used as concentration camps, where men would be piled up to be peed upon and traumatized.

The soldiers would kick them as if practicing karate and spit on them. Men would be beaten repeatedly. The prison in Ljubuski was horrific, as were others across the state. The cells were infested with mice, and the basement was flooded and kept for *"special"* people. The prisoners who, before the war, held professional careers like police officers, doctors, and lawyers, were treated no differently than the common rabble. The basement had one window, and guards would urinate through it on prisoners.

Prisoners were fed a piece of bread at best and executed at the *"Christians"* will. *"But what crime have they done?"* I would ask myself frequently. Their only crime was to be of Muslim faith. Ljubuski was predominately a Christian community. The town where I come from is just a five minutes' drive from Medjugorje, a huge Christian pilgrimage, where they claim Mother Mary showed herself. People from all over the world go to visit that place to be closer to faith. I wondered why Mother Mary didn't show up again in the middle of this hell we were in. Even God had turned his back on us. Muslims and Croats were driven-out of their homes and exterminated in the northern part of the country, to make space for the Serb population. The mandate of that time was, 'Create all Serb Towns' and the same was being done by the Croats in the south. All three religions walked away from this war with bloody hands. To explain this level of craziness is difficult to put into words – but suffice it to say that everybody suffered. People from all three religions were made refugees due to the war.

Something was brewing in the air. You could feel it, like

that gut feeling that something terrible was going to happen, yet you cannot quite lay your finger on it. Radio stations announced a curfew would be implemented for all citizens, so anyone caught outside past dusk would be immediately arrested. The authorities knew that the victims were the ones making rounds in the dark in search of either sustenance or escape. Most businesses closed in Ljubuski, and only the Croats got to keep their jobs at the beginning of the war. This further added to the distress of the other minorities. Money was no longer available in the banks for anyone to withdraw. Those in retirement stopped getting their pensions. The more the war raged, the more it became obvious that others were losing jobs, not just Muslims at that point. It was a matter of time before all of the food resources would be used up. Even electricity was cut, and food resources were dwindling to the bare minimum. The first initial weeks without electricity trundled on by, but months without it in a state of war was an unthinkable, unfathomable situation.

People began burning their furnishings for a source of heat and the ability to cook what little food they had. We would wet our books and then place bricks on them to dry them straight and hard, so they could act as fire starters. It is astonishing to see how creative the human mind works in times of desperation, transcending into survival mode. People mixed grass with water to trick their stomachs into believing it was food. We Bosnians were mastering the art of trickery and illusion, deluding our bodies into believing all that was being provided was actual food and light in order to survive.

Snipers killed those who ventured past curfew and left their bodies to decay for weeks before family members could get to them. That stench of decay does not leave your nostrils no matter how hard you try. The entire ideology behind this violence was to remind us that we were all soon going to be dealt with in the same manner - the only difference being that if we disobeyed them, we would be assassinated faster.

Across the state, horrors of entire families executed at gunpoint spread like wildfire. Mass graves began forming with minefields around them, so families could not get to their loved ones. People were beheaded and soldiers kicked their heads around like soccer balls. Thousands of women were raped and kept in cages like animals. Some got pregnant from this horror and gave birth in camps, and then chose to kill their own babies so they did not die at the enemy's hands.

A fellow refugee shared with me what she witnessed while placed in a concentration camp. A prisoner in labor was giving birth when the male soldier walked over to the pregnant lady and ordered the child to be placed on the floor with the umbilical cord still attached. The male soldier then stepped on the newborn child in front of her mother's eyes. How helpless the mother must have felt cannot be expressed in words. To grow a being in your womb for 9 months, and suffer excruciating pain giving birth to it, only to watch it be killed the moment the child first wails - it conveys the savagery embedded in the war.

This was the fate of us Bosnians. We were perceived to be dust and hence made to mingle with the ground forcefully. Even before the children had a chance to bloom, they were squashed brutally. No one was spared an ounce of mercy. The horror of how vicious, wicked and heartless this war is equivalent to the Holocaust, and cannot be summed up by this one mere incident.

The city of Sarajevo suffered the longest siege of a capital city in the history of modern warfare. The siege lasted 1425 days. Snipers and the Serbian army surrounded the city, ensuring that it was left without electricity, food, water or ammunition to defend itself. 490,000 grenades fell onto the city and people died of hunger, explosions, and snipers.

Memorial to children killed in Sarajevo City. The names are etched on the cylinders

A few blocks from my grandmother's house, up the

Zabljak hill, was a charity place where donations of food and clothes from all over the world would arrive through the Red Cross. On the first Thursday of every month, a line of women and children would wait for small packets of food. I would go with my grandmother. It was an uphill climb that lasted about 20 minutes. It was a humbling experience, to say the least. Those that would arrive later in the day would risk missing out on food, as only so much was given out each time. My grandmother would gently pull on my hand, making sure we were walking as fast as our feet would take us so we would not be late and miss out. During a typical three-hour wait in line, we wondered if we were going to be one of the lucky ones. *"How much longer grandma?"* I would ask impatiently, shifting my weight from one leg to the other.

The army by now would have taken the good rations from it, and we would get the rotten food. We were being deprived of the little sustenance rendered our way ever so graciously by the rest of the world. We would queue for three hours' worth of wait, just to have palm-sized servings of expired food products. Our Catholic friends from Hercegovina would pass by with their families and watch us stand in line as if we were animals in a zoo.

They would just be spectators of our miseries, the people who we once deemed to be our friends. To them, we were nothing more than amusement now. Their parents were not separated, but allowed to keep their jobs and did not need to wait for food at the beginning of this war. I would hide behind my grandmother as I stood in line, embarrassed when I would see them. I pretended that it was not me, but someone else that they'd seen. It is hard in situations like this to not feel like a circus freak. I remember being ashamed of myself as I did not want for them to see me begging for food. Yet I had to. This was the only source of food for myself and my family. The food was old, and they would not allow us to have the fresh products that arrived. We would stand in line, receiving updates on the demise and torture of our kin and kith. This was how we heard what was new, and what the army was going to do next. It was a useful way to keep all of us victims in the loop so we could be prepared for the next set of attacks.

A lot of people lacked electricity, batteries, and food. We would share information with each other and overhear all this. Standing in line for food would allow us to learn who died in the past month and who was able to escape.

Women would share all kinds of things with one another.

"Did you know that Mujo was killed yesterday?" Mujo was Esma's father - Esma was a friend of mine who went to school with me. A good friend, you could say. The one who I thought no matter what happens would be there. I thought of her so much. I did not know where my father was, either. Will we hear the same news about him from one of these women? All sorts of thoughts would occupy my mind. I always hoped that someday, I would get to know how he was. I prayed that one of the women in line who had radio and batteries would maybe someday hear about my dad as they knew him. Then I would get to know of his whereabouts, too. The ration we were granted was of typical food packets, containing a small bag of flour, rice, and powdered milk. My grandmother was such an innovative cook. You would not believe the things she would make with this stuff. Receiving one of these packages was like winning the lottery. It meant that at least for a couple of days, we would have food. Upon our arrival back to my grandmother's home, my job was to go through the rice and pick out all of the little black bugs that would be crawling through it.

This was a gross job initially, but I grew accustomed to

doing it. I was quick to understand and appreciate the value of even this. Powder milk did not even taste like milk. We tried hard to break the clumps in it, but they would get stuck in our throat every time we swallowed them. It was disturbing, but we accepted it thankfully, as many did not even have this. The only certainty in our fate was of bleak oblivion. Even the option of desertion was filled with a thousand hindrances due to the heightened security throughout Bosnia and Hercegovina and its neighboring borders. Each night, I would go back to bed, where darkness cloaked even our shadows. We were afraid of making the slightest bit of noise, as even that could have been enough reason for our deaths. I only knew two things back then: darkness and fear. The first family member we lost during this hell had been arrested about the time men were being separated from their family members and taken to concentration camps. We decided to meet up with our family for a couple of days to decide what to do and where to run next.

The war's situation was only deteriorating with each passing second. We had spent a couple of days in *"Bascina"* little village on the river Trebizet, which is about a ten-minute drive from my grandmother's house. It was a vacation home and land that had been in my family for generations. My family tried to figure out where to run. We had arrived in the afternoon, right before curfew. We spent the evening in the dark, careful to not be noticed that we were there. But no one slept that night.

That night, in particular, was crazy. It's amazing how fear magnifies every little thing. Even owls and crickets seemed a threat to us that night. Our brains were making hallucinatory catastrophes of even the sounds of nature. Someone was coming after us or hiding behind the bushes - such was the paranoid thoughts of our mind. We only tossed and turned in our positions, not daring to close our eyes even for a split moment. Our guards were up. Vigilance was the virtue most useful to us if we wished to survive.

Unsure if the police would arrest us, our nerves were on edge. That evening, every noise outside seemed as if it was a threat. That night seemed longer than any other night in my life. But as soon as the sun came up, I wished we were still hidden in the dark. The sun-exposed us to a horror gift-wrapped for us to unwrap. We stepped out of our front door to see a black garbage bag just lying there.

The elders scurried outside to bring it in. If only they knew the revelation inside the black bag, they would never have dared to rip apart the garbage bag. Inside of it was our family member, in pieces with wires wrapped around his wrists. He had been tortured in the camp and then cut up to pieces. It was a gruesome sight for anyone to see, much less a child. This was a message for us. They were aware of our hideout and that we needed to get out at the earliest. Our only chance of running away was once again challenged. But all the horrid thoughts had to be set aside at the sight of the pieces of our dead family member. The elders decided to provide the remains with a proper burial, which created the next stings of dread. How? The cemetery was located in the middle of the valley, which was now surrounded by snipers. If anyone were to go there, then they too would be in need of burial. After much contemplation, the elders ventured by themselves as we children had already witnessed more than we should have. However, much to our surprise and relief, all those who had gone to bury the deceased came back alive. I guess the police only wanted to instill fear amongst us so that we would not think of seeking refuge elsewhere.

This time, the police devised the same schemes of collecting all the women in the same area, much like the men previously. They sent repeated messages about the need for women to get themselves registered when in truth it was for their convenience. We heard all the women would be picked up by the masses and taken to women's concentration camps as well. This was it - it was time for us to flee our own country, too.

Our first plan of action was to seek safety. After all, fleeing a war-stricken country is difficult, especially when you are targeted by the enemy. The idea was to seek refuge and shelter at a local monastery in Ljubuski. This was the same monastery that saved my grandmother from being executed by the Germans during WWII. Perhaps that was the reason we expected the same kind of treatment from them.

However, when we pleaded for safety and asylum, we were kicked out, without them even considering the possibility of granting us protection. It was an act of cruelty, made all the more potent because they were ardent followers of Jesus Christ. They prided themselves in their undying love and belief in Jesus Christ, yet what did they do when presented with the opportunity to save and spare someone's life?

They chased us out of the monastery – the House of God. Their treatment made me often question if Jesus Christ would agree with their decisions, with the senseless killing and forcing people out of their homes, their country. My belief is that there is one God - whether I call him Jesus, Allah, or Buddha. God, or whatever his name is would not have done this or even allowed for this to happen. I strongly believed, at that time that HE would not have agreed that people use HIM as an excuse to kill and create this hell on earth. My aunt picked up the ten-year-old me, and with my stepmother and grandmother, we headed towards Croatia. If we got pulled over or stopped at the border, we were not to speak as our accents would have given us away. We picked Catholic names as we were going into a predominately Catholic country. I picked the name of my childhood friend, Maria.

Maria was of the Catholic faith, and I wondered where she was. I wondered if she still thought or worried about my safety, as I did for hers. She did not have to escape because of her religion at first. See, this war was ethnic cleansing on Muslims, and even though we never entered a Mosque nor knew how to pray, our names were Muslim and that was all that was needed for us to be captured and executed. Nothing else apart from our names. Did we deserve to be exterminated in this way, much like you would exterminate cockroaches?

I questioned why we were so insignificant that the world did not care to intervene. They only watched the fiery flames engulf us into ashes. Mass graves and concentration camps made me wonder if there was more to the ethnic cleansing that happened during that war. The rape and murders as well. It was the bloodiest war ever since the Holocaust in Europe. People were treated more like cattle than humans. People fought for the little food they had. Bosnia was forced to crumble into nothingness. The once scenic land was now just a sight of pity for the world, but no one came forth to stop the misery we were in. And my questions went unanswered, of course.

No one spoke in the car. We just sat and looked out the window, all lost in our thoughts of securing a safe passage. The Bosnian curvy roads and rolling hills made me carsick, but I tried to look out the window and keep my mind focused on something different. If I squinted my eyes to the right, I could see my reflection in the glass. And the sight shocked me. If I had seen this image in a crowd of people, I would not have recognized myself. I had never seen my face look that way before - elongated, distorted, as if I was looking through a reflection of moving water.

I had never feared for my life before either, and perhaps it was that fear that began misshaping my body. Before I was a reflection of pale skin clinging against my skull, with no emotions apart from fear. I held on to that thought only for a minute and had to release it quickly - it got my heart to race and fear to begin taking over. Fear was a well-known emotion to me by now that I had grown accustomed to. The car moved through a wooded area, a section of the road that I had not quite remembered until this moment. Tall evergreen trees passed us by, one after the other and then a patch of deciduous trees painted in bright red and orange colors appeared. Fall, my favorite time of the year, had arrived. It was a time when all the trees shed their leaves and released all that was accumulated during the past season. It was that time of the year when we see the beauty in the death of things. The thought of this occupied my mind. There was no beauty in the brutality unleashed on Bosnia. The death of the people was the exact opposite, as this was a sheer monstrosity.

As we approached the border to Croatia, my nerves began to get the best of me. Dead silence engulfed the car, and the only sound you could hear was the sound of the car engine and our escalating heartbeats. I closed my eyes so tightly that the skin around my eyes was wrinkled. *"Be still,"* I repeated in my head. If I was still enough, we would be safe. My heart raced so fast that it seemed I had just run a mile. Sweat beads accumulated on my forehead and I noticed one broke free, rolling along the side of my face. I wiped it away quickly as if I was wiping a tear. I thought that if the patrol police were to sniff fear radiating from me, they would catch on our ethnicity despite our pretend identity. The sky was gloomy, and thunder clouds hovered above us. Rain. My favorite weather element. I loved to listen to the roars of thunder and rain. Something about the drip-drop resonating in the mass of space was consoling to my heart. The sky opened up, and big raindrops began bathing our fast-moving car. Clear drops of rain rolled down my window. Maybe God was crying, the ten-year-old me thought. Perhaps he was disagreeing with this hell that we were desperately trying to escape.

We reached the border sometime in the afternoon when the day shift guards left and the night-shifts guards were on a break. Maybe the rain chased them away, or perhaps God intervened and made this miracle happen. The one thing that we were sure to battle, the one thing that we were preparing for, was what we were going to say when we are stopped by the border police. But when we reached the border, we found nobody there. It seemed way too easy. We crossed the border with no problems and reaching Croatia meant reaching a bit of freedom.

We were left with no choice but to leave behind our house, our belongings, our identity, and even our names, to embark on an unknown journey. Pushed out of our town for fear of being taken to concentration camps, we crossed the border into Croatia, where we were homeless for close to three years. For some time, we hid out in people's homes.

The first home was in a scenic little town in Croatia. We had family there. Eight people in one house, unsure of how we could afford enough food for all of us. I did not realize it then, but this is where our refugee life began. Under no circumstances could we go back home for fear of being killed. Adults don't share much with children in situations like this, which is a pity since it leaves the child to use their own imagination and come up with all sorts of scenarios as to what would happen. This first little town was only a stopping point for us. Unaware of where my father was, I worried if we would ever see him again.

I made friends with some kids next door to us who were also refugees. The back of our house was enclosed by a large concrete wall so we could play there without being seen. As typical children, we played out what was happening in our lives. And so frequently, we played war. Throwing rocks and hiding behind makeshift bunkers was our way of playing out our reality. One of those rocks hurt the neighbor's kid. It hit him in the forehead and opened a large gash on it. It could have been any of us that threw the rock at him, but I got blamed for it. I was an easy target. By getting in trouble from these people we were living with, I was not allowed to go to the basement when the sirens went off. This was my punishment. The light in me was fading. These horrors became the shadows to my light.

The first time the sirens went off after this incident was life changing for me. The wailing of the sirens ripped through the empty streets of this scenic little town in Croatia. Its howling sent chills to my spine, like a pack of wolves ready to devour their meal. It was a lot like sirens that ripped through Ljubuski when the war started. Everyone ran to the basement, and here I was, sitting on the couch. I could hear the sounds of the planes approach us.

I could hear explosions. But I just sat there. Not being allowed to run to the basement made me wonder what my dad would have done if he was here. I folded my legs underneath me and stared out the window. Fear immobilized me, and even if I were allowed to run, my legs would not allow it. In the distance, thick smoke was rising from where the bombs had gone off. Random gunshots in the distance made me wonder who was shooting; who was the target of the untamed bullet and would either of them find me? It was all the same to me, whether I survived or died. I had never experienced feeling as alone as I did at this moment. I was so easily disposable. This situation was possibly the last time I had ever played as a child. But God spared my life, and I just sat there watching out the window.

I was glad that this first refuge was not our permanent stop. I was happy that I was no longer being blamed for a casualty another kid was inflicted with. But neither were any of the other homes permanent. In a situation like this, a child learns how to not be seen or heard. It was a lesson that was hard to break in my adult life. As an adult, it is important to learn how to stand out, especially when it comes to the work-setting.

We learned to live in fear and obey others while hiding out in random homes. This meant sitting down and not, under any circumstances, walking by a window, for fear of being seen and reported. For fear of endangering the families that had graciously invited us into their homes. A period of several months followed where we bounced from home to home.

Most of those three years, though, we hid out in a just about abandoned village at the base of mountains in Croatia, just north of Split, a beautiful oceanside town at the top of Adriatic Sea. The place harbored terrible living conditions, yet I had grown fond of it by the time for departure came.

We arrived at the village in late fall, 1992. The road continued to climb up the mountain, curving to the left and then right, like a snake before it is ready to strike. Small stone built homes in the state of disrepair began appearing alongside the road. We arrived in the early morning hours to not be noticed by anyone. The car stopped and we stepped out. The mountain air smelled clean, and then the silhouette of a man stepped out from behind one of the homes. I could not quite recognize the shape of this person. From the distance, I could see it was a man of medium height, skinny and slumped over. We walked closer to him.

I squinted my eyes and recognized the face. My father's medium stature and bright white hair that was plastered to his head...they were unmistakable. I could not believe my eyes. For a second, I thought I was hallucinating. I stood and stared for a minute, not believing it was him. Then my thoughts channeled their own voice. *"Dad!"* I screamed with excitement.

I ran up to him as fast as my legs would carry me. *"DAD!"* A laugh mixed with a cry came out of me. He signaled me to be quiet and not yell. But a big smile was on his face, and open arms hugged me tightly. My dad was here. My dad was back in my life. He was safe and alive. My only dream after years of torture came true, and for the first time in a long while, I felt what it was like to smile freely and be present in the moment than just dread.

Only two families lived in the village, an elderly couple and a single bachelor who had inherited his home through the family. Our temporary home had its roof caved in. Much of the village was that way. Around ten homes, and only two were occupied. These medieval homes were typically constructed in the same fashion, featuring a kitchen, a bedroom, and a potty outside.

Those old stone construction homes, worn from the years and the harsh winters, still stood erect as if they were tombstones to ancestors that lived there for thousands of years. The roof had not caved in from bombs but from years of not being lived in. We were grateful for the walls though because they were able to cut down on the wind that would rip through. However, just because the village was abandoned did not mean that we were free to roam about the place, and we hid out in the house or the woods. Each car that would pass along the road meant we had to run inside and hide. Still, despite the odds, this became a safe haven. Here I was reunited with my father and eventually brother. No longer did I want to sleep with the fear of never being able to be united with my family.

My father was wise and would build a fire only during specific times of the day so that we were not noticed by anyone passing by. He would put bricks in the fire, and let them heat up. Once they cooled enough, we would then wrap these bricks in our clothes, and this would keep us somewhat warm throughout the frigid cold night.

But, for the lack of a better word, we starved there. Scavenging for berries and picking fruit trees was our only hopes and source of food. We grew up accustomed to hunger. Not the hunger when you skip lunch during a busy day, but the hunger that painfully echoes through the shell of your body. The kind that makes your stomach cramp up. It was a miracle that my family and I made through each day. I guess we were fueled by the relentless hopeful prerequisite for survival.

We could not stay there unnoticed though and eventually, the two families figured out our existence. My father made friends with a middle-aged man, Nediljko, who lived there. He was a large man with quite a sense of humor and would frequently bring smiles to our faces, breaking through the ever-present fog of fear and worry about what would happen in the future. He named me *"Black"*, for my long dark black hair. Nediljko became one reason we looked forward to each day. He had a way of befriending even the little ones, that is, me and my brother. We had found someone to share our lives with, someone who did not pose a threat towards us. He would stand on top of the stairs and yell my name out loud. It did not bother me, as he was a kind man and I loved seeing him for the smile he was sure to bring to my face.

I missed home though. I would often think of my childhood friend, Maria. Did she think about me? Was she okay? I missed my home. I wondered who was living in our house now. Did they think of us? Did they feel comfortable in another person's home? My mind would drift towards my mother's belongings, and I would wonder if any remained there. Would the new residences keep them or discard them? I bet they did not know how much her clothing meant to me. I bet they had no idea what it felt like to flip the pages of her notebook, with her handwriting and random drawings. I bet they had no clue that there was a little girl who used all of those things to feel closer to her mother. A mother she would never know. A mother that was such a mystery to her. These things that meant nothing to them, but meant the whole world to me. My only connection with my mother, the only thing that would allow me to be closer to her. The only priceless inheritance I had left.

I remember our first winter in the village. There was no snow, but a cold wind would rip through often. The roof, or what was left of it, leaked rain inside and magnified the cold. That winter, Nediljko brought two chicken drumsticks for the four of us. Oh, our excitement was as if we had just won the lottery. We knew it was more than winning a lottery. The sight of food that wasn't the bits we found in the wild elevated our demotivated spirits.

We circled around the plate: my dad, stepmother, brother and me. Two drumsticks for four people, and yet neither of us fought with the other. I did not take my eyes from them and could already imagine what they would taste like. My mouth watered from the thought of the chicken against my taste buds.

Then my father spoke. *"What should we do? Should we eat it today or save it for tomorrow?"* I thought about that question for some time. Do we devour these drumsticks today, or do we go to sleep tonight knowing that two drumsticks would be on the menu tomorrow?

"Leave them for tomorrow, Dad," I screamed out with

excitement, even though my stomach growled, begging to differ. This meant that we would have something to look forward to tomorrow, rather than be dejected with our mundane routine now. We needed something good for a change, so the thought of having chicken tomorrow got us through the horror of today. I went to bed that night with so much excitement - much like the excitement kids experience when it's their birthday the next day, and they cannot wait to celebrate with everyone.

This was one of the happiest moments of my childhood. The following day I woke up super early. The sun had not yet come out. Antsy with excitement, I laid in bed thinking about chicken drumsticks. My mouth watered at the thought of it, much how a dog would start salivating when it's about to eat a bone. When the first sunrays of light came through and lit up the room, I began shuffling in the bed, hoping to wake the others. I tried to occupy myself as long as I could, to have the day go by in high hopes. That day, in particular, was very cold. I could see my breath in the room, but my body had created a little warm border around me, and the thought of crawling out of the clothes I had piled on top of me made me cringe for a minute. The heated brick that was next to me was just about cool to the touch, and I pushed it off the bed. It hit the floor and made a loud sound. Perfect. What a perfect way of waking others. I was unable to contain my joy.

That afternoon, the moment we all waited for was about to happen. We placed wood behind the house and started a fire. Smoke arose, and there was nothing more soothing to me than the sound of wood crackling in the fire. I sighed with satisfaction at the random little pops and sizzling and white smoke going through the air. We no longer had to hide the fire, as the two families in this village were aware that we were there. Little red coals of wood began forming with a thin coat of ash around them.

My father placed the two chicken drum sticks on to start cooking. Oh, the aroma of chicken drum sticks in the fire was invigorating, lingering in the open air. It did not take long to cook them. Two drum sticks for four of us. What a treat; such a vast difference from what we had been eating until this point. We divided them into four pieces. I inspected mine for a second. A crunchy bit of skin that had burn marks from the flame, followed delightfully by some of the meat. I chewed it fast and swallowed it, but then regretted not savoring it for longer. And just like that, our first proper decent source of food in forever was gone. The second winter in this place was worse than the first. It seemed as if the sun would set at noon due to the position of the village, which was at the very base of the mountain.

We had grown accustomed to the cold for the most part. At this point, my father had made multiple trips to Split to fill out papers with the UN for refugee status in any other country in the world that was willing to take us. He would do manual labor for our friend Nediljko, who would give us any spare food he had. My father did everything in his power to get us to safe and healthy living conditions. And surely, with our endless trials and tribulations, came the sun with rays of hope shining onto us.

After about a year on their waitlist, we were notified that we were accepted by America. The next step was health checks in Split to ensure that we were healthy and free from any infectious disease. We arrived at Split by 12, with an hour to spare before our appointment. We crossed the street towards the building we needed to be in. Two UN soldiers in their uniform stood at the other side. The sight of them made me grab my stepmother's hand and squeeze it tight. I feared people in uniform at this point. To me, these people cloaked their identity behind a uniform to hide their evil deeds. They were engaged in a conversation between themselves, carelessly laughing. Their sight made me wonder what could have been that funny. Where were they from? Oddly, it felt weird to hear others laugh. Here we were, hoping to survive, and others were living their best life.

At that point, I badly wanted to be someone else - someone whose life allowed such laughter and carelessness. I did not want to be this frightened little girl, afraid of how the day would unravel, wondering whether I will lose more of my dear ones. We walked into the building and checked in with the secretary. We must have been a sight for these healthy people - emaciated, tired and hungry. They separated us into two different rooms - one room was for men, and the other was for women. I went with my stepmother to the right towards the room for women. We entered a hospital-type room with a divider.

Six other women of various ages were already there, impatiently waiting. The doctor and his nurse were behind the divider.

He gave us instructions to strip down. Without question, women started stripping down while I was in complete terror. *"Strip down,"* he demanded. My thirteen-year-old self was devastated at this moment. My body began shaking at the thought of exposing my body to a stranger. *I don't want to do this,* I thought to myself. I was not comfortable with this body that I had grown into.

"Hurry up," the doctor repeated impatiently. I remembered the moment in the basement when my pants were inside out, back home when the war hit us. The embarrassment I felt then was nowhere near this moment, and I trembled in fear. *"I don't want to do this,"* I thought to myself.

The deep stern voice reiterated, *"I don't have all day. Strip down now."* He intimidated me into meek obedience. I stripped down, attempting to cover my emaciated body with my hands. He made me walk towards him, grabbing my shoulders with a strong, irritated grip, and twisted my body towards him. His breath reeked of cigarettes. I opened my mouth, but no words came out. His look pierced me, and I tried to look away. *"Now walk to the wall and back towards me,"* he ordered sternly. I knew I had angered him by not obeying from the first instance. My eyes were focused on the floor as I was too afraid to look up. I did as he said - walking first to the wall and then back towards him. I stood in front of him, shivering from cold and from fear. He ran his large hands through his unruly black hair, pulling it away from his strong forehead. A dark shadow of mustache framed his thin upper lip. He had deep-set dark eyes that studied me with repugnance. *"You will learn to do what you are told,"* his voice, stern and deliberate, escaped his mouth. The heat from his breath prickled against my skin.

My body had broken out into goosebumps. My hands were trying to cover me. Once again, he grabbed them and threw them to the side. *"God where are you?"* If God could raise Lazarus from the dead and part the red sea for Moses, then he sure could make a miracle happen in my situation. He sure could make this stop. How was this a medical checkup when all the doctor was exploiting was helplessness? His voice sent shivers down my spine. His callused hands felt as if they were ripping my skin. I looked at the nurse that was helping him, but it seemed she deliberately avoided eye contact with me. Disgusted and irritated, he yelled, *"Get her out of here."* I shook at the sound of his voice but felt a sense of relief that my *"exam"* was done. I believe at this moment that I wanted to die. I was using all of my strength at that moment just to breathe.

To be taken advantage of just because of your identity was burnt like the town you belonged from. Was this the medical check-up mandatory to find a shelter? After the appointment, we headed back to the village. The wind carried the smell of damp earth.

The sense of being used was overwhelming. I stared out of the car window, feeling violated and embarrassed. I was happy to go back to the village. At least nobody knew me there. Nediljko had picked us up with his car, as he had some business in Split. *"Why are you so quiet, Black?"* he asked, but I was too embarrassed to even talk about it. I stared out of his car window, biting my bottom lip, attempting to keep the tears from escaping my eyes. I gulped down the lump forming in my throat multiple times so that no one else could exploit my weakness.

Our last year in the village was a miserable one. That last winter was by far the toughest. Years of homelessness and hunger began wearing our bodies down. We learned that America was going to take us and that we were leaving in May of 1994. I found myself already starting to miss this village we had grown accustomed to. I sure would miss Nediljko. What a fantastic friend he had been through these past three years. The thought of saying goodbye brought tears to my eyes. Who would put a smile on my face when we left? The village had become an integral part of our life, and no matter how hard life was there, we were still considered human.

We were treated like people who felt pain. There might not have a proper roof over our heads, but we had the freedom to breathe. Our neighbor had become an angel, and his smile gave us an unknown reassurance, and I knew this is why I would miss this village. Our last night at the village was rough. Nediljko and a few friends we had made joined us for the final goodbye. The moon was so big that night. I don't think I ever saw a moon that big. It lit up the courtyard of our home. The moonlight danced around that night. It illuminated Nediljko's face, who at this point had grown to love us.

I watched him quietly, attempting to remember his face. This kind man, who had done so much for our poor desperate family, was missed dearly already. He was a good friend. He was the best. We had nothing to offer him but manual labor, yet he offered us so much in return. I will never forget him. This was the last time we would see him. I did not know then, but I began grieving the loss of him, of the village, and of my home. Leaving this place seemed surreal.

Would I ever see him again? Would I ever visit this village? I bit my bottom lip and attempted to hold back the tears. I blamed the smoke from the fire for getting into my eyes as I wiped my tears. I just could not seem to get past the lump in my throat. This lump that prevented me from telling Nediljko how much he meant to me, how dearly he humbled me, and how he taught me to give life another chance.

Morning arrived sooner then I wanted it to. We packed our clothes in one bag. I turned back to look at the house that we had lived in for the past three years. I strangely missed it more than our home in Ljubuski. I looked at the stairs where Nediljko would yell *"Black"* so many times. As the car pulled up the windy road and towards Split, I whispered, *"I will miss you."*

We said quick goodbyes in front of a bus. The sound of wailing could be heard for miles. Loved ones were saying what seemed like a final goodbye to those of us heading to another world. Whether it was for the better or worse was yet to be determined. A world where there would be no shooting, no death, no decaying bodies, no bombs, no belongingness, and no home. It seemed unreal. We boarded the bus to Zagreb. I was never good at riding in a car or bus. My motion sickness would get the best of me. We found our seats on the bus and headed out.

Our long trip to Zagreb began, and we reached in the early morning hours the next day. I stared out the window, much like those men in Ljubuski did when they were taken to concentration camps. *Where are we going? What is this new life I was about to begin?* I wanted to cry, but I didn't. It felt like I had no more tears left in me. But it seemed like my soul was crying. It was grieving for all the loss I had incurred, and all the nightmares etched in my mind forever.

A random deep sigh escaped my body. My father and mother sat behind me while the bus was moving quite fast. It felt as if it was almost leaning into each turn we took. And with that, my stomach swayed from one side to the next. Nausea was building inside the pit of my stomach, and I made myself close my eyes. I no longer needed to see anything around me. I pulled a piece of bread wrapped into the paper. My stepmother made us pack this before we left.

Maybe this piece of bread would soak up the bile rising in the back of my throat. I ate it with my eyes closed and shortly after, drifted off to sleep. No nightmares or sweet dreams, just darkness and the rhythmic pattern of my heartbeat.

Piercing screeches shrilled through the drive. I woke up after nearly getting jolted out of my seat, around 5 am. The sensation of flying forward got me to grip the armrest and hold myself back so I don't fly face first into the seat in front of me. I turned quickly to my parents, attempting to get a reassuring look from them.

"What is going on?" I asked, turning towards my father as if he would know the answer.

Men in uniform came on board then, demanding papers from everyone. *"Papers!"* they screamed loudly. The sound of military boots against the bus floor echoed in the pre-dawn darkness. They walked with agitation and purpose, making me shrink in my seat. What if they took away my family from me once more?

People began digging through their belongings, pulling out pieces of paper to give them. *"These are refugees from*

Bosnia," said the bus driver to one of them. A woman who was sitting next to us with a small child, clearly in a panic, began screaming out. *"We are not armed. We are refugees. Please let us go."* A soldier grabbed her by her hair and threw her on the floor of the bus. Her son threw himself at her attempting to protect his mother from these monsters. I covered my ears with my hands to attempt to keep out the wailing. Her sobbing was getting louder as they dragged her off of the bus.

The screaming of the little boy could be heard even when they were thrown on the pavement. The gunshots stopped their crying. A thorough search of us lasted about 30 minutes. To me, it seemed as if it had taken hours. Finding nothing illegal, the soldiers eventually unloaded from the bus and allowed us to make our way to Zagreb. Nothing else was heard except the bus engine increasing speed and taking us away. We reached the outside limits of the city shortly after 9:00 am, my vision filled with tears.

***

Thinking of it now, my brain is still protecting me from living through the atrocious horror of back then. I cannot put enough of what I saw into words. I cannot stop expressing what it was like to be victimized and treated as an object. Mercy was a nonexistent term then. What was mercy? A myth for the victims, that they clung to until their last breaths. A myth, a fable, where we Bosnians imagined the life of peace and security that was taken from us by force. We were forced to suffer consequences just because our religion differed from the others. Infants and elders alike were graced with a similar fate of barbarity. Where no one stepped forward to salvage us from the inhumanity inflicted on us daily.

Three years of cold and hunger, fear and desperation eventually got us to the United States as some of the first refugees to settle in Twin Falls, Idaho. We gained nothing from the war in Bosnia. Millions of our people were dispersed all over the world. Bosnia continues to be corrupt, with no jobs and no opportunities for young people to even make a living unless you have money and can buy yourself a job. You read it correctly. Buy yourself a job. How absurd. The corruption continues, and the beautiful place we once called home is slipping through our fingers.

Chapter 3
A Mortal Wound

"Dad, how much longer? I am tired and I don't think I can travel anymore." I turned to my father desperately, jet-lagged and exhausted from the trip that had taken nearly 48 hours, including the layovers and a night spent in New York City when we reached American soil. A disapproving look from him made me turn back around and be quiet. We were all tired. Tired and curious about this new place we were coming to.

We arrived in the U.S. at the end of May 1994. The extent of my English was limited to only a few words, and I was unable to put even a sentence together to save my life. The final stretch of our journey was full of drudgery. A small plane we boarded in Salt Lake City seemed as it was going to crash from the sky. Beneath the majestic wings of the aircraft were fields of open land, with signs of crop circles all around.

Turbulence throughout the flight had left my stomach churning. The man sitting next to me was lost in his book, as he paid no attention to the turbulence of the plane. My fear and squirming in my seat went unnoticed. *If this plane comes crashing down from the sky, will Nediljko know that we did not survive?* I occupied my mind with all sorts of random thoughts to keep nausea at bay.

Amidst the turbulence, I recalled one of my lessons from Geography class back in Bosnia. I had learned about Idaho and the famous potatoes grown there. My thoughts were lulled by the turbulence, which seemed as if it was hushing my repetitive thoughts of arriving in Idaho and picking potatoes on a plantation.

I was certain of our future. I had learned about slavery in America back when I was leading a normal life in Bosnia. That is when it clicked. *Why else would these people bring us to their land?* Our own people had exterminated us and kicked us out. So why would someone else care enough to bring us to their country? What use were we to them if not for enslavement? We landed after a tiresome journey, only to be met by the refugee office staff at the airport and transported to the apartment set to be our new home.

A large white bag with blue letters on it made us easily identified and exposed our harsh reality to the rest of the voyagers. All of our paperwork had been placed in it so that we would be noticed by refuge personnel. We walked out of the plane and set foot on American soil. The quietness of the surroundings was unsettling to our ears. No bombs were going off. No snipers were killing people from the skyscrapers. No sirens. No village. No Nediljko. The thought made me feel unnerved. It was as if something was missing. Just quietness that felt antithetical to haphazard state I had grown accustomed to.

It took me time to adjust to this peace as I had learned to embrace the sound of sirens blaring. The sirens back in Bosnia warned us every time a new threat arose. What was going to warn us here? Certainly, there were no sirens. Here we could only rely on ourselves - a concept that was very strange to me at this point. When I embraced calamity, I was to forget all the brutality as mere fragments of my imagination and accept tranquility. However, my mind and soul were dubious. Surely, there was more than what met our eyes then.

Our refugee placement was a cozy apartment furnished adequately and equipped with a fridge full of food. The sight of all the food seemed like a mirage. I was, after all, starved for a long time, and had forgotten what it was like to have food at our disposal. I scarfed down a banana, not being able to remember the last time I had one. How odd was it to find such satisfaction from something as simple as a banana? Greedily, I plucked the biggest one from the bunch and stripped the peel away in a frenzy, to expose the once familiar pale yellow flesh of the fruit.

I kept the piece of banana in my mouth for longer than I needed to, simply to savor the taste and rich, creamy texture, pushing it side to side with my tongue before finally swallowing. The yellow peel, tainted with more brown spots than yellow, fell limp to the floor. I gained a disapproving look from my parents that made me quickly bend down and pick it up. I knew they wanted me to value each and every morsel, but not to disregard the luxury of having food. As I disposed of the peel respectfully, I smiled to myself, remembering Charlie Chaplin's black and white movies, where he would slip on banana peels on purpose just to make others laugh.

Tucked in the comforts of the refugee apartment, we watched OJ Simpson's white Bronco being chased by police on the TV. Oh, how grateful we were to have moments of peace and serenity once more! We were safe together, away from the monstrosity lurking free back in Bosnia. That is all that mattered. The first day, despite being a refugee, I was relieved to be in the company of my parents and brother in a place that I knew was protected from damnation. No bombs, no gunshots, no violence to shrill and disrupt the calm of the solemn evening.

We had brought one bag full of clothes for the four of us from our last safe haven and that was it. We had not opened this bag since the village. I unzipped it and pulled out a sweater I would wrap bricks in before going to bed. It still had ash stains from the fire on it. The feel of the rugged wool in my grasp transported me back to the last night we were there. I grabbed the sweater with both hands and pulled it closer to my face. I inhaled as hard as I could, so that my lungs were full of memories, engraving the faint fragrance of wood and earth in my mind. I could smell the fire on it, and sense how hard my father had to struggle just to ignite a source of warmth for us.

The tears brimming in my eyes started pouring down like a waterfall. I missed the village. I missed Nediljko. In my head, I recalled the events of our last night there and remembered the shape of his face. His large protruding nose, deep-set dark eyes, small forehead, chubby face, and those large teeth sticking out. He was my friend. A friend that looked past my Muslim name and saw me only. Me - the child who did not know where she belonged to. One of the *lost ones* who had no home, no country, nothing. My identity was no longer intact, and every time my mouth wanted to betray my presence, I had to hold back thinking of the catastrophe that would have befallen on us if I had made the simple mistake of saying my own name.

My whole family and I would have ended up paying the hefty cost of that. We had nothing now. But we felt rich because we were safe and together. That is all that mattered. This stuck with me through my adult years too. A lack of material things did not profess a poverty-stricken state, but lacking the basics of shelter and safety did. To have your loved ones suffer a tragic demise was what made me feel poor. As a result of all the never-ending savagery, I witnessed in my childhood, I was saved from chasing things of monetary value. Life taught me that no matter how much stuff you have, it can be taken from you with the blink of an eye. Things do not matter to me. People matter to me. Henceforth, I wanted to cherish and live every single second of each day with my loved ones. Time mattered to me. Time, the most fragile possession of ours is the greatest currency we have. Time with our loved ones is what is priceless. No amount of worldly treasures can turn back time. I learned to live fully in the moment. This moment, when you are reading these words, will pass and not come back.

At any one given moment, you could move mountains or you could waste that time. If you have the liberty of moving mountains, then do it, instead of sitting idle. Seize it instead and do what matters to you. Do not just waste time, because when you are on your deathbed, there will be no more chances. No more 'do-overs.' When time is lost, you cannot reverse it and you will be left with remorse of not making the most of it.

The refugee center signed us up for ESL (English as Second Language) classes. Learning English was essential to our survival. It was essential to me as well. Learning it would mean I would no longer be picked on or laughed at in school. Learning the English Language was to be my salvation from bullying, as it could change how people perceived me, making me a normal human being in the U.S. There is a huge misconception that those who do not speak English enough are not smart enough, and perhaps if one is to speak or yell louder, then this would make us understand what they were saying. We got yelled at a lot. But yelling did not make me understand what they were saying any better. It just made me think that these people had short tempers, and that yelling was acceptable social behavior in America.

We studied hard day and night, and after about three months in the U.S., my brother and I began talking in English. At this point, we were not fluent, but we could find our way around and communicate with others instead of looking all around us with fear-filled eyes. Despite not being fluent, this was a moment that every refugee child could appreciate. It is, after all, the first step toward attaining normalcy.

The one when your parents start bringing all kinds of papers to you to translate for them. You feel empowered, capable of being treated like a human. My father and stepmother found jobs almost immediately. We became contributing members of our community and that made us proud. It made us feel connected to our new surroundings; we didn't have to feign a sense of belonging. I still missed the village though, and Nediljko. Despite the comforts of a heating system and the thick brick walls, despite a comforter to cover myself with every night, I missed building fires to warm up, and the feelings of a warm brick wrapped into my sweater at night. I was thankful for a proper roof above my head instead of the thatched one back in the village, but I missed the subtle sound of the dew drops resonating in my head. It had been a lullaby. The hell we had escaped in Bosnia had not gone for me though.

Although I was in a safer place, far away from the horrors that I lived in Bosnia, they had left their vivid imprints on my memory. Post-traumatic stress disorder is very much real. Being safe did not erase those years of trauma. Even time seemed to have faltered on its healing ability. We learned not to speak of it. By staying numb, we gave off the impression that we were ok and that the tragedy has ceased to exist. Alas, we were far from being ok. I live with trauma every day of my life. Even if I mock normality in broad daylight, I am plunged in the undertows of my misery within the shadows of the night.

Some of these scenes still replay in my head vividly, and I have learned to live with it. It has become a dark passenger of mine. A shadow that casts itself on each happy moment I encounter in my life, preventing me from being happy when something good would happen in my life. My soul forever mourns the irrecoverable loss of Bosnia that I witnessed first-hand. The horrid screaming of victims still echoes in my ears and leaves me sweating at night.

This is the true state of most refugees. The nightmares for some of us have not stopped since the 90s, yet we have learned to function and live a relatively normal life. We are scarred, yet we have survived. We have become resilient in the deepest pit of hell. We fled the clutches of the demon rummaging through Bosnia. And we soldiered on. After being broken and scattered on the ground, my father and stepmother were swift in picking up their pieces and putting ourselves back together to secure our only chance of safety.

We were welcomed by a community where most befriended us upon our arrival. On a few occasions, we encountered people who believed that refugees suck up the resources of their community and should be shunted back to the dungeons they came from. My father had a year to pay off our four plane tickets. With dust specking his pockets, he worked relentlessly to do that. Both he and my stepmother worked day and night so that we could pay off our tickets. Any aid we were to be granted was suspended upon the employment of my parents. Contrary to popular belief, the U.S. government did not give us cars, bungalow, or an enormous sum of money. We were furbished adequately to carve a new life for ourselves from scratch. The urgency refugees feel to make something of their life is stronger than what most American people experience. In a way, we had to catch up. I attribute this to the fact that we had to start from absolutely nothing to make something of our life. We had a bed to sleep on and a door to bolt us for security, but to establish a new beginning, to have a life once more, we had to buckle up our own shoes.

We were uprooted to this new place that looked very much different than where we come from. No skyscrapers, just one-story homes looked perfect. The front yard had the greenest grass I had seen in a while. Perfection was the face of our new community. Empty streets would throw us off, unlike the once bustling ones of Bosnia. Grocery stores were brimming with food that was untarnished, taint-free, and gleaming. I had never seen apples so big before my first shopping trip in America. No one walked around the town. It resembled a curfew hour we had in Bosnia during the war. The first year in America was rough. We were to adhere to a new lifestyle and get accustomed to a brand new culture. Everything presented a cultural shock to us, but we had to suppress our surprise and adjust to the way of living of this new land. We assimilated the best we could. We even learned to eat peanut butter and jelly sandwiches. One could buy peanut butter with jelly already in the jar. We did not have peanut butter at home back in Bosnia. We ate peanuts but peanut butter was a whole other delicacy, one my brother and I were growing fond of.

My parents were unable to afford brand new clothes, so we wore hand-me-downs. The only time this bothered me was when children would point it out at school, laughing at our misfortune. I think, compared to the rest, we were poorer than poor. We made sure to shut the lights off in the house when we went to bed or when we left home to avoid a big bill. We already had new laws and rules to abide by, a new school and a group of friends that could not imagine the hell we had escaped. But we also had to adjust to our altered financial situation. We tried everything in our power to save each and every penny my father and stepmother could afford to give us.

People in the US would go to the movies and watch a story similar to what we lived through, attempting to understand where we came from. However, to us, our trauma was more real than what they saw on a big TV screen or Hollywood production. No movie, no matter how beautifully scripted or played out, can depict the actual fatality the victims suffer. No movie can highlight the pain and never-ending torture we refugees face, where each moment prickles the threat of death against our skin. My stepmother worked at McDonald's in the kitchen and my father worked at the College of Southern Idaho washing dishes - a job he held for 10 years before he retired. These entry-level jobs provided us with the basic necessities of life.

People tend to avoid such jobs, due to the fear of imposing ambiguous threats to their social status. My parents, however, had no choice. To us, even this was a blessing, one that we embraced with gratitude instead of resentment. At least, we were graced with another chance. Most of the victims in Bosnia had not even procured an opportunity to escape. We had lost all we had in Bosnia.

Everything that my father worked so hard for. The home that had been in the family for generations. The condo where my biological mother first brought me and my brother from the hospital. Where she kept books and journals. The home where she lay sick from breast cancer and eventually died. We lost the house that had absorbed our laughter and tears, the walls that were a witness to our festivity and loss. Most of the photos of our loved ones were gone too. Years of our life were erased so quickly. All was gone. It was as if our whole life was just an illusion. We no longer existed in that country. Our identities were massacred, much like the Bosnians. We were forced to abandon our joy, our sorrows, our pride, and our tomorrows. My stepmother was a wonderful woman who took care of us the best she knew how.

Like any other woman, she too must have had expectations and dreams linked with her marriage to my father. But how ungrateful had life been toward a selfless and devoted woman like her! She took pride in her job and I can't help but wonder how humbling was it for both of my parents to spend their life working hard to move up, only to have it all taken away and start back from the very bottom. Never once did they complain about how tiring their journey was. My step-mother was an incredible wife. She was my father's strength and pride, holding him up whenever his knees gave up and walking hand in hand with him to give my brother and me a better life. She taught me the value of appreciating things that are not glamorous in life, such as an entry-level job at McDonald's. It did not matter what you are doing as long, as it is honest work and you give it your all. After all, at the end of each day what lulls a person to sleep is peace of mind and not an over-priced comforter.

***

After arriving in the U.S. under the refugee program, we thought life would finally compensate for all the years of grief we suffered. But our happiness was, once again, short-lived. My stepmother was diagnosed with breast cancer in 2002. I cannot imagine how scary this must have been for my father. To have life strike his second wife with the same horrible disease as his first. Her health continued to fluctuate for many years, taking a toll on her strength and physique.

Every piece of good news from the doctor's office

would be celebrated; it would elevate our spirits with newfound hope, and we would reassure one another that eventually our stepmother would be fine. Each piece of bad news, however, was greeted in fear and dread for the next day. Somehow, we wished for time to pause at the moment. Gradually, we learned to live in fear once again. We rode the roller-coaster of ups and downs for years, clinging on the ropes of faith for our step-mother. After all, she was a wonderful woman whose strength was prevailing. But in December of 2006, the doctors stated that her cancer had spread to her brain. This terrible news brought us face-to-face with the new harsh reality. Until then, we had been pushing aside this fear that had been creeping on us, but now it leaped and stood arrogantly in front of us. We were advised by the doctors to be prompt with the surgery if we wished to avoid regret later. Shortly after, we made a trip to Boise for surgery.

The day of the trip was adorned with the typical Idaho winter - 120-mile stretch of highway from Twin Falls to Boise, a trip that typically takes about 1.5 hours took close to three. I was pregnant at that time, at the stage when you start sporting a protruding stomach. This to me was the most beautiful part of pregnancy, when you can proudly flaunt your belly. My stomach was almost touching the steering wheel that I was gripping strongly. Ice covered roads drove my nerves over the edge; it was extremely difficult to maneuver the car properly. The atmosphere in the car didn't help my nerves either, the tension thick enough to be sliced through.

On cue, Christina Aguilera's song 'Hurt' came on the radio. I had to bite my bottom lip to keep my tears from slipping, else I knew I would not have been able to make the drive. I still can't listen to that song as it's associated with the unspoken emotions I faced that day. Our car desperately tried to push through the fog to make it to the 2 pm appointment with the neurosurgeon. My mind strangely recalled the moment we first escaped Bosnia and the car ride to cross the border to Croatia.

This moment felt no different to that. After all, we were trying to escape this doom and reality of her cancer, hoping that the surgery would be able to take care of things and put my mother back into remission. I did not want to lose her - not this way at least. She had already suffered endless agony. She deserved to be laid to peace at the end of her journey, void of all pain. Cancer only afflicted her with excruciating pain.

Fog engulfed our vehicle, and the thick snow made for dangerous driving conditions. I could hardly see past the front of my car. We were driving into the unknown, unaware of what road conditions laid ahead of us, much like the fate of survival of my stepmother in her brave battle against cancer. I don't know how we made it to Boise that day when our minds were so wrecked, but we did it, despite the odds against our favor. Perhaps it was because of the silent supplications we all were making for the sake of my stepmother's well-being. The surgery went well in terms of removing the tumor from her brain. She now sported a scar running from the middle of her forehead toward the back of her head. It was her battle scar - a verification of her strength to surpass the toughest of trials life had put forth. However, this surgery took away the person I found to love and cherish. She might have fought to prevail her illness that had spread like poison in her system, but the poison had killed her will in the process.

Her personality was different now, and she became more reserved and quiet. The woman who was once the life of our household was now uninterested in conversations, mostly staring off in the unknown. When asked what she was thinking about, her only curt response would be

'Nothing.' Including her in family activities was difficult, and we recognized that the person who came out of the surgery was no longer her. This new person was strangely familiar, but we were no longer able to connect with her. This disease was draining her mercilessly of all dignity. It drained her of the ability to care for her family, something she used to take pride in. She started to isolate herself from us, her loved ones, who were always there to hold her from falling. Her nausea and pain became the new normal. She would wheeze in short breaths of air due to the fluid in her chest, like an asthmatic person attempting to breathe. Breathing eventually became more noisy and difficult for her. She slipped into a worse phase of distress than ever. Ever since the surgery of her tumor, it appeared she was attempting to separate from us somehow. In my belief, this was partly due to cancer and post-surgery, and partly an attempt on her part to prepare to enter the last phase of her life.

The woman who was once an epitome of strength, who never accepted defeat, had now shunned the idea of a new tomorrow. Our relationship with her changed significantly too. Previously, to whom we used to run just to be engulfed in her warmth radiating embrace, now a mere act of affection such as hugging felt indifferent. We hugged her as if she was a porcelain doll, being careful not to squeeze too tight, so we didn't break her. We were more afraid of interacting with her. To have her withdraw from us was crippling us from within.

In July 2007, my mother came to see my newborn daughter. I had not seen such excitement lighting up her face in what seemed like ages. It was so good to see her holding my little Yasmina as if she was holding a little doll. This image is seared in my mind with the most permanent inks. This was the happiest I had seen her in years.

The goodness of her soul was too big for her body. Post her surgery, I thought we had forever lost our guiding light, but when she cradled my daughter in her arms, I saw the faint speck of light restoring in her eyes. At that moment, my heart brimmed with joy at the chance of getting back the only mother figure in my life.

My stepmother holding my infant daughter. This was about a year after her surgery. You can notice a scar running from the top of her forehead towards the back of her head

On September 10th, 2008 at 9:15 A.M., I visited my stepmother in the nursing home where she was placed. In the past year, her health had deteriorated drastically, to the point that tending to her ourselves was out of the question for her well-being. We desperately wanted to keep her home so she could be comfortable and surrounded by people that loved her, but her cancer had once again spread to her brain. Only this time, it initiated grand mal seizures that left her falling on the floor, making it difficult for us to lift her up. We were terrified even to touch her, petrified that a single touch of ours could aggravate her condition. With heavy hearts, we decided to place her in a skilled nursing facility known as Canyon Rim. Canyon Rim overlooked a beautiful canyon and Snake River and provided its patients with a much-needed boost of tranquility. This facility became our second home, and we spent all of our waking moments there with our stepmother. It was about the time that a big Mormon temple was being built in Twin Falls, a few blocks from Canyon Rim.

We watched it rise from her room, and I wondered if God was watching this beautiful structure grow. God - the only one who could make everything okay at this moment. The one who I have reached out to in my prayers on and off in my life. He was sure to hear me this time. This time would be different. This time, I was praying for my stepmother, so how could my prayers not be accepted? Maybe the building of the temple, right before our sight was meant to signify something, whether it was to hope my stepmother would recover or to trust in the planning of God.

At the time, I was working as a substance abuse

counselor and had to attend a Drug Court meeting with the judge and the team. I would come to see my stepmother like clockwork before I had to rush off to work. That day, the hallway toward her room seemed even longer, and the more I walked near her door, the further it inched back. Something felt different, but I could not put my finger on it. I found a nurse in her room as I walked in. A middle-aged woman, who must have been in her early sixties, was bent down toward my mom's bed. She was gently working with her, suctioning secretions that had collected in the back of her throat. In truth, the nurse was supervising her death.

Her hair was pulled up in a messy bun, signifying that she had been working all night. She did not initially acknowledge me as I walked in as she was occupied with my stepmother. I shuffled my feet loudly in an attempt not to scare my mom. She turned to me and noticed the worry on my face. She pointed to her hands that had started turning into a deep purple color. What threw me off was her distorted breathing pattern. Her 54-year worn-out sick body was helplessly lying in bed. I was not sure what was happening. Although somewhere deep inside me I knew that she was dying, my soul desperately prayed for some type of miracle. I prayed for healing. I was certain I would be a witness to a miracle that would heal her body, and she would join her family again. But it wasn't to be. This strong woman who loved life so much was robbed of her strength. Each second was depleting her soul. She loved giving gifts, and would always come back with a little something after a trip to the store. The only gift I could gift her at this tender time was nothing more but my eternal love.

I came closer to her bed and whispered, *"Mom, it's me."*

I still recall the warmth of her cheek pressed up against mine. Her breathing was heavy and loud. I watched as the nurse squirted morphine into her mouth.

"I have to go to the Drug Court meeting, but I will be back right after that, ok?"

I looked expectantly at her, only to be dejected by her lack of response.

"Don't be afraid, mom. You will be ok," I whispered softly to her. *"Thank you for choosing me to be your kid. Remember, when I sat in your lap asking you to be my mommy? That was the best thing I did in my life. The best choice I made. I chose you. Say hi to my biological mom if you see her. Don't worry. If you have to go, it's ok. I will*

take care of dad. I will miss you with every fiber of my body. I miss you already. I love you so much, mom. You have been the best mom. Thank you for everything. But don't go until I come back. Don't go alone. I will be back in an hour, ok?"

Tears flowed uncontrollably down my face. A lump in my throat kept me from swallowing, afraid that if I took my next breath, my mother wouldn't take hers. The clock in her room was particularly loud, each tick-tock indicating the impending doom in the room. Oh, how I wished I could smash that clock into a thousand pieces if it would only make the time stop from taking away my mother. I needed just a little bit more time.

A little bit more time to prepare for what was going to happen, to pray a little more, to beg God not to take away this blessing from me. But time stands still for no one. The tick-tock quietly spelled out the final moments of her life running out, and there was nothing I could do to stop it. I was as helpless as the nurse, but at least she was doing everything within her means, with the equipment she could use to relieve my mother of her pain.

The light in her room was dim. A hospital bed pushed up against the wall, and two big windows overlooked a patch of grass and trees. The stench of sterile equipment reminded me of being in a hospital, alerting my mind to the harsh reality unraveling before me. Memories of all the surgeries and hospital stay we'd had in the past started flooding in. Each memory was lucid and slowed down my heartbeat.

I thought to myself for a second - *is this the room she will die in?*

The sounds of the call lights beeping loudly in another patient's rooms echoed through the hallway. Someone needed help from the nursing staff. We needed their help too, but there was nothing they could do to help us. Nothing to resurrect my mother's soul, tie it to her body, and lift the burden of pain from her. I sat with her quietly, laying my head next to hers. This surely served the purpose of letting me feel her next to me before she would embark on a different journey alone. *Will I remember this moment? This special moment of her still in my life?* The sounds of a busy hallway outside faded into a hush. The only sound resonating in this room was of the damn clock ticking away, along with the erratic beating of my heart as an eerie reminder of what the future holds.

I intertwined my fingers with those of the woman who chose to be my mother after my biological mother died. A woman who spent her life raising two children that were not hers. A woman who loved me with her whole heart even when I did not love myself. I held her hand, inspecting it hard enough to burn it into my memory. The heat of her palm made my hand sweat. Her hands were still warm; surely this woman whose will was undeterred could fight for her life...but this would have meant she would have suffered excruciating pain endlessly.

Life had been cruel towards her, towards me, and our family. I wiped my sweaty palms on her blanket and then slid my hand back. The sound of the loud clock reminded me that I needed to go to work for an hour. I tucked her in for what would be the last time. I pulled the blanket over her, as her heart beat faintly like a flickering flame of a candle, about to burn out.

I leaned in, kissed her sweaty forehead, and rushed off to work. The faster I reached there, the faster I would return, and then maybe my mother would still be there. The Drug Court meeting that day was typical. We discussed the client's progress. I managed to find the right opportunity to tell the judge that my mother was not well and I had to keep my phone on just in case. In my head, I questioned myself what that case could be. In case of what? In case she died. I had to reassure myself that she would not die, that a miracle would happen, and we would all be okay. My goodbye to her was unnecessary, and she would soon be okay. I can feel it. I was reassuring myself to delude my mind with hope. Maybe that could trigger a change of events where my mother would have recovered, and I would banter with her about today's court proceeding. I walked into the courtroom with my team.

As we sat down, the judge said, *"It is September 10th, 2008, time and place for Drug Court. It is four o'clock."* As soon as the judge said those words, my phone rang. I remember my heart beat had escalated, and I felt the blood rushing through my body. I grabbed the phone and ran out of the courtroom, ignoring the disapproving looks the judge must have sent my way.

My voice trembled as I said, *"Hello"* only to be torn by the answer from the other end.

"Your mother is gone," said a somber voice. *"I am sorry."*

Somewhere deep inside me, a tremor began building momentum, vibrating as it spread through my body. It reached my chest and then my throat. It formed a lump in my throat, preventing me from saying anything. My mind had gone into denial, numbing my senses before I began choking on my words as a sob erupted out of me. Violent spasms overtook my body and I shook all over. She had been there at all times throughout my life, she was there, and I was not there for her at in her last moments.

I had abandoned her when she needed me the most. I felt the ground beneath my feet to violently snatched away from me, and I fell into a plight. I missed it. I had wanted to be there for her, and yet I missed it. She died in that room alone and I was not there. In her time of need, I was not there. The sense of guilt kicked me and echoed in my hollow body.

I don't know how I made it to Canyon Rim Estates in Twin Falls. All I remember is running back to the courtroom, making so much noise that I got a disapproving look from the judge. All I know was that I had grabbed my purse and bolted outside. I ran down the courtroom building, a guard yelling at me from behind. Perhaps he thought I had done something wrong. The sound of the busy traffic around me registered in my head like it was coming through a tunnel. I don't quite remember the drive to the nursing home. The only part I do remember is when I made eye contact with a man next to me at a red light. Our eyes locked. I must have had a desperate look on my face. I wondered if he could tell that my world had just stopped. Could he tell that I had just lost one of the most important people in my life? Cars around me were rushing to wherever they were going.

Rushing? To What? Life continued on for them, while my world had stopped. I don't remember the rest of my trip. I don't know who took control of my car. I don't know how I got to Canyon Rim Estates. My mind was stuck in a loop where the rest of the world was placed on mute and the life had played the cruelest form of trick on my mind.

That September afternoon, the sun shone brightly as I found myself parked in a panic, unsure how to switch off my car. My hands were rattling against the car keys.

Frustrated with myself, I abandoned my car ignited to just be by my mother's side. It seemed the simplest tasks were hard for me to figure out. In spite of my hands trembling and my legs shaking, I took the next steps heavily. In a pure state of panic and despair, I ran inside and down the long hallway toward her room.

I was met by the nursing staff, who yelled and ran after me. One lady grabbed me from behind, placing her hands under my armpits and pulled me backward.

"Let me go to my mom," I screamed.

I struggled against the firm grip of the nurse as I felt my own strength betray me at that moment. Perhaps my body knew it was wiser for me to fully accept the bitter truth of my mother having left us.

My short battle with them ended when one of them stepped right in front of me and screamed, *"You have to wait until we clean her up. Your father is on his way here."*

Neither of us wanted to be screaming in the middle of the hallway. The commotion had caused other families to gather there. The nurse's words registered in my mind. My father...the thought of him stopped me in my tracks, and I ran back to the parking lot to see his car pull up.

He swung his car door open, only to collapse on the ground. I screamed at the sight of him. For a second, I thought he was dead too, and I dashed toward him. I picked him up and hugged him. No words were said as we held each other and cried. Neither of us was sure how we had managed to drive when our hearts were full of grief and aching at our irreplaceable loss. They say people die as they lived. She had lived life very gently, like an angel whose presence was felt. Like a gentle whisper of wind, her aura was to forever linger within our souls. Her soul departed her body to be free from its endless sufferings. This shell of the body lying in this sterile room was no longer her. Her face had a similarity, but the tenderness that was once etched on her face was no longer visible. She was gone.

I replayed that suffocating scene in my head a thousand times. Why hadn't I die in war? If I had, then this moment, this worst moment imaginable, would have been seen by me. It seemed as if the oxygen in that room was gone, and no matter how hard I tried to breathe, all I did was gasp for air. Every time I saw her motionless body, I recalled how her skin would crinkle around her eyes she would try to focus on something, how her lips would stretch seamlessly to flash her mesmerizing smile to us.

A smile I would now never be able to see. The wind outside of her room picked up, causing me to shift my gaze from the earthly remains of my mother towards the window. I noticed the leaves that were ready to fall danced carelessly in the wind. At the face of their death and the seasons to come, they danced. How could they be merry when they were about to perish, just like us humans? They made me wish for us humans to do the same, to rejoice in the time of death rather than mourn endlessly. Not to fight this inevitable moment that looms and waits for all of us. Did this wind attempt to carry her gentle soul wherever we go when we die? Or does our soul rustle against the teasing breezes when it's free from its vessel?

We watched as Mike's Mortuary Home staff put her on a gurney and covered her. I physically gasped for air as I watched those strangers load her up in the back of a hearse as if she was nothing more than an object. It strangely felt as if she was being kidnapped. But this was it; her body was vacant of mass and of her that they were taking away till she was placed to rest.

In my head, I was screaming, *"Wait, I am not ready*!

Where are you taking her?"

The voice in my head gained the power to form the words, and then those words escaped my lips.

My voice shook as I yelled out, *"Wait!"*

But what did I want them to wait for? To have them stop would not turn back time or awaken my mother. She was asleep for an eternity now. Then what would calm my shivering soul that was craving the sight of her upright and healthy? A prayer? No! The one thing I prayed for did not come true and my world was shattered, much like the sky shatters in the reflection of a wild river that is flooding everything around. All life in me was numb. Soundless, piercing screams were trying to escape my blood, yet my body had lost the ability even to budge a muscle. I felt weak. She was 54 years young. I stood under the awning at the back of Canyon Rim estates and watched them pull out of the parking lot. I cannot express the trauma I experienced at that moment, and the subsequent traumas of grief I felt a million times thereafter.

I was 28 years old at that time, feeling like an orphan. How could I have ever prepared myself to lose my support system? My mother, my hero, and my shining light at the end of the tunnel was no longer there to watch my baby grow or to comfort me in the future. How could anyone prepare themselves to bid their parents goodbye, no matter how well-versed we are with the fact that all of us are mortal? The demise, even of our loved ones, is inevitable. That night as the sun set, darkness fell heavy and embedded with suffocation. It engulfed me. That night, while I lay in my bed, I felt the same coldness my mother's body would have felt in the mortuary freezer. My heart suffered a mortal wound that day. I experienced the worst type of crying imaginable - the silent one, where everyone is asleep, and it begins to build at the base of your chest, climbing upwards to the top of your blurry eyeballs. This type of crying requires you to hold your breath and grab your stomach and mouth to keep quiet. My heart was constantly clenching and unclenching vigorously at the hurt, and I had to halt myself from forming more tears. They were already bloodshot and stinging with the unshed tears, but I had to hold back from breaking down once more because I knew in the pitch darkness of night, I would not have been able to comfort myself now.

Realizing that I won't be able to sleep, I got out of my bed and sat alone in my dining room at the table. My home was as silent as the village in Croatia where we spent three years homeless. I held my head in my hands, feeling my veins pulsing violently under my fingertips. Silence rang all through the house, except for the panting of my 13-year-old Pomeranian Jack. Jack always knew when something was not quite right. It was about midnight, but my mind was wide awake with a million different thoughts. My head was caged in my hands, eyes closed as I slumped over the table as if I was reading something. But I was not reading. My eyes were closed, but that did not matter anymore. I no longer needed to see things around me. I just needed to feel them. To feel this loss of a mother, not once but twice in my life, was a pill hard to swallow. But life had mercilessly shoved this pill down my throat.

How helpless are we to watch our beloved die right before our eyes? No matter how far mankind has advanced, we still do not harbor the power to resurrect back life into our loved ones. My mother was gone right before my eyes, and I watched the whole ordeal helplessly. I mourned not just her departure but the fact that I hadn't been by her side when she needed me the most.

I thought I had made her take a vow, to wait for me so I could be there to hold her hand. I told her she was free to move on and maybe, just maybe, she needed to move on. That is why she did not wait for me, and, in my absence, took the final flight by herself. This was her strength. She knew that neither of us would have been able to see her body jerk for the last time before her soul escaped her body. And this is the only reason that I found comfort in.

I mourn her loss every day. She was my mother by choice and she made me who I am today. I will forever be in debt of her selflessness and her devotion to us. Hence, the only consolation I found was in accepting that it was time for her to think of her betterment for once.

Chapter 4
The Color of My Grief

At this point, my life split into two parts, life before my stepmother's death and life after her death. It was like a mile-marker, a pivot point for me to use and measure everything against it. Life before this loss was insignificant. All of the tragedies of my life – the loss of my biological mother and my living through war – dimmed compared with this new trauma, that I had not only to acknowledge but also integrate into my life hereafter.

This life turned into a constant reminder of my life in Bosnia during the war. When I was hopeful about my life turning a new tide toward a shore, it only capsized my journey as I found myself in a similar circumstance all over again. I do not quite remember the days following this loss – the heart-wrenching, soul-crushing loss of my adored stepmother. The only memory that left its imprint was the image of her fading breathing pattern. Anything else leading to her death - the doctor's verdict, work, and home – they do not exist in my memory. I know that my grief immobilized me thereafter.

This grief penetrated deep into each cell of my body, shutting down my mind. Taming it seemed impossible. All I was able to recall was how my mother was no longer here to hold me or comfort me. The thought alone was enough to hitch my breath, and when a waterfall of tears cascaded down my cheeks, I lost more control over myself.

All I wanted was to turn time around at any cost and have my mother back. The result of my wanting the irrecoverable was me drowning in despair. I made myself helpless and unwilling to pour my heart out to another soul, even when people tried to reach out to me. But how can they have known the storm emerging from within me?

Soon my grief started to impact my life for the worse. Sleeping was as big of an issue as waking up was. It was like I was re-experiencing this loss. It felt as if I was in the deepest, darkest pits of my hell, suffocating and dying a little every day. What was worse was my frozen limbs had given up, crippling my ability to crawl out of the hell I was crafting for myself.

This became a horrid norm for me - six months of severe night terrors. Repeating dreams haunted me. Even when I tried to fight the demons haunting me, I would awaken with a jolt, drenched in a pool of sweat and misery. One such nightmare that I am still unable to erase from my memory involves finding myself buried in the coffin with my stepmother. A candle was blazing brightly, but threatening to burn out any moment, and I was desperately trying to put her decaying body together even as it kept slipping from my grip.

It was like a race against time. I could feel my hands trembling. And as the candle would burn out, I would wake up screaming. In another dream, I would wake up in a home with a man that I did not know. He was so tall that I could not even see his face. This mysterious man was leading me toward a small home where a woman was stirring a pot. I only saw the woman from the back, cloaked head to toe. As I approached her, I pleaded with her. *"Please pray for me, I need your help, please pray for me."*

She would turn her face toward me, and her jaw would dislocate itself and elongate, much like the mouth on the mask from the movie Scream. She would let out a high-pitched scream. The next thing was me falling off the edge of a canyon.

I could hear her laughing and yelling. *"I put a hex on you!"*

I would wake up screaming and crying hysterically, not comprehending whether my dream was a fragment of my imagination, or if this was reality. In other repeating vivid dreams, demons would growl and circumambulate my bed, but no matter how much I tried, I could not open my eyes. I had no voice to scream out. I tried to pry my eyes open with all my strength, but nothing would work. Even my own voice did not find the strength to come out. The dreams felt lucid, and I would experience each and every tremble in my veins.

In these dreams, I would clutch my infant daughter tightly in my arms and closer to my chest, to keep the demons from taking her away. These dreams ended no differently than the other horrendous nightmares of mine, and I would wake up panicked. I would frantically search for my daughter, only breathing when I would find her tucked safely in her crib. My house validated I was just suffering from a state of sleep paralysis, and that I was a victim of my own raging thoughts.

However, as hard as I tried to fight for peace, my battle continued on each night. My terrors seemed so real that I found myself scared to go to sleep at night. I resisted finding comfort in my own bedroom. I despised the thought of rest, and whoever advised me to rest was labeled my enemy. How could they suggest that I simply go to bed? It was easy for them to say - they were not the ones suffering, so how could I expect them to provide me with a profound solution? This was just the bitter poison seeping in my system. It came from losing myself slowly. I perceived my own family and friends as inconsiderate people, making me feel disgusted with everything.

Six full months of terrors and I was at my wits' end. I wanted to get out of my own skin. Perhaps, that could satisfy the demons who were after me? To simply take my life...that felt like the easiest option, to put an end to this drudgery once and for all. The only thing holding me back from committing such an act was the sight of my daughter. She needed her mother and her sanity. I continued to fight what seemed like a spiritual war for the sake of my daughter, and to liberate myself from the hell I was trapped in. Even then the thought of being punished constantly gnawed at my heart. Why me? What sins had I committed in my miserable life to deserve this? Six months of hell, of me barely holding on to my job as my exhaustion settled in. The lack of sleep combined with my continuously jumping at everything started to affect my work quality, as well as my ability to pay attention to my house and family. Even when I wanted to comfort myself by seeking shelter in work, my composure would be eroded by the demons. Dark circles painted themselves permanently around my eyes, and an ever-present haze clogged my brain's ability to focus. I was just a tired soul trying to figure out how to stop this hell and escape.

That was when I thought if I started to pray, maybe the Divine would be able to resurrect me from this purgatory. In spite of everything - my desperate attempt to believe in God throughout my life - I was no further from Him then the Devil himself. Over the course of six months, I was only able to close my eyes for no more than three hours before I would wake up terrified. After enduring this for six months, my strength was fading, every bit of my will depleted in my fight to get out of this slump. Death seemed merciful than to go through another day of weariness. I resented waking up the next day.

While each new sunrise meant a new beginning for many, to me it meant another day for the horrendous nightmares to replay themselves. These dangerous thoughts emerged within me against my will. I was left alone to fight this battle within myself, as no one around me was able to understand my woes. Over time, in hopes of trying to preserve my sanity, I began learning how to embrace this darkness that engulfed me. After all, it was the only consistent thing in my life. After accepting that I lived in a vicious cycle of endless nightmares, my eyes started adjusting. I began seeing friends for what they were – a waste of time and a source of destruction.

No one is there for you, except for their own selfish means. People pretend to be there for you in your weakest moments, but they only seek perks for themselves when you're at a high. This became a new way of punishing myself, where I blamed myself for being alone and others around me for not being sincere. My thoughts comprised of me reprimanding myself. If only I prayed harder, if I tried harder to find new doctors and new treatment, this would not have happened. I would have been sleeping as peacefully as anyone else around me.

It was the 6th of March, 2009. My bedtime routine was ingrained in me by this point. I knew my mundane routine better than I knew the back of my hand. It started with turning on all the lights in the house and waiting for my husband to come home and patiently enter the living room, even when my eyelids were heavy from lack of sleep. Back then, he worked at Con Agra and would end his shift at midnight. This meant he would come home anytime between 12:15 to 12:20, depending on the traffic. I had grown accustomed to recognizing his car engine, as he would make the final turn toward our street toward our home. I would be slumped over on the couch waiting for him to come inside so we could go to bed. This was all to avoid my bedroom if I was alone at home.

I had started to blame my house and my bedroom for instilling fear and nightmares into me, rather than admitting that maybe my mind was responsible for my suffering. I knew very well that these nightmares would happen no matter where I was; they would follow me even in the loudest and brightest of places. It was not my environment - the problem was within me. We went to bed that night, as we did every night before this one. My heart raced erratically at the thought of the terrors that haunted me.

"Let it be not so bad, please."

Out of desperation, I would repeat this like a mantra in my head. I would lay in my bed, glued to my husband, as I felt safer with him. I would keep my eyes open for as long as I could, knowing that at some point, I would wake up in fear, screaming. The more I stayed awake, the shorter the night would be. The shorter the night, the less time I would spend being stuck in my mind. There was nothing I wanted to do more than put as much distance between myself and the difficult situation I was captured in. I felt shackled, unable to fight against the Devil who cast a shadow on me each night.

Me, shortly after my mother had died in the midst of grief.
Captured by my husband as I was planning her funeral

That night was no different than any other, in terms of me panicking and wishing to be able to survive without sleep. I stayed awake as long as I could, staring at the ceiling anxiously. Each second, I waited for the old grip of fear to grasp my heart and soul and tug me into fright. However, later I realized that night had been much different than any other in the past six months. I am unsure of what led to this dream. Maybe it was the mercy of the unseen that graced me.

I had a dream that I was lying on my bed. My bedroom was lit up so brightly that it was blinding. I looked much younger than I was in real life. On the headboard of the bed, an eye opened up and what I believed in my dream was God's voice declared: *"It will be ok, my child. Everything will be ok. This is your light in this room. Don't forget it."*

Had it been the same shrills from the woman who claimed to have hexed me, or the demons dancing around me, my body would have been trembling. Instead, this dream led me to spread my limbs and let the comfort of the mattress below seep through to my worn-out muscles. The bright warmth of sun rays against my skin woke me up on March 7th, 2009. I opened one eye first and then the other. It took my eyes a minute to adjust to the brightness of the sunrays. Feeling at ease, I turned over in bed and noticed that my husband's side was cold, hinting that he had already left for work. My clock in the room read 10:27 a.m. Surprised and puzzled that I had slept until late in the morning, my thoughts ran over the dream I had. I got up as quick as I could and rushed to the living room. For the first time in what felt like ages, I was not scared to wander around my house. I was able to breathe freely without any worry or unease.

Up until this point, I did not quite believe in God, as I was raised in a house that was not religious. I did attempt to believe in Him throughout my life and wanted desperately to have some type of proof that this whole God thing was real. The dream that I had last night left me further dwelling on God. What was that dream? Was it my mind coming up with fantasy, attempting to pull me out of my hell in hopes of comforting me? Or was there more to it?

What was more surprising was that my terrors from that point stopped. Was it all a coincidence? Maybe. Or was my battle over? Did I win this spiritual war taking place within my mind for the past six months? Did the devils try to make me surrender my soul, or did something wipe their existence from my life? I was not sure at the time. A million thoughts were raking my mind, but more importantly, I was beyond relieved to be able to be at peace.

With time, I realized that even if there is a God, we still choose to interpret the world around us in whichever way we want to. We either surrender ourselves to a deity controlling our affairs or maneuver our lives according to our worst fears. My battle was far from over. All I did was try everything within my power to run away from my nightmares. I resorted to comfort myself by choosing to believe that this was God stepping in. Whoever He might be, it was a decision I had made, as everyone else does at some point in life.

This was the saving grace that pulled me from the deepest and darkest nightmares imaginable. At least this was what I chose to believe. But my grief was still far from being over. Having successfully emerged from this storm, I was clueless to what more awaited me. My relief was short-lived as my grief once more took a plunge.

***

I grew up in a house that did not believe in God. I questioned His existence and chuckled at people who spoke of His mercy, His miracles, and His divinity in most situations up until this point.

"What a joke," I would often think to myself. What kind of god would allow this to happen? In a world full of sex offenders, murderers, and evil-doers, he had chosen to take away my mom in this undignified way. What kind of god would allow wars to happen? My world was left profoundly empty. I chose to doubt god instead of finding a reason behind all these events.

I failed to realize that my resentment toward religion

was aggravated because of my own experiences. Having been forced out of my own country just for our names, having lost my mother when my brother and I were too young…these were the reasons I strongly disbelieved in religion. Maybe there were people who could have assisted me in handling my mother's death in a healthier manner, but I gave in to my heart's weakness.

Without her, I was lost, only misplaced my identity along the line. I had chosen to bury myself in my work at the time, as that was the only escape I could find where there was no reminder of my loss. After all, a distracted mind is one that focuses on everything that is unimportant, just to avoid things of priority. I surrounded myself with people who would assist me in this distraction rather than help me cope with my mother's death.

It was easier to ignore the pain than to tend to it. They served my temporarily need and I was content with this. I found myself lost in crowds of familiar faces, lonely in this social experiment of mine. Despite being invested in these relationships, at the end of the day I was empty. Hollowness encompassed my soul. I wanted something but could not identify what. I found myself in this self-inflicted coma and was quite unsure what would bring me out of it.

Alas, I was left tossing and turning restlessly, thinking of ways to conceal the pain rather than to heal myself.

A new person tried to emerge from me after I was successful in suppressing my hopeful self. This person was able to see clearly how family was only there to provide support if it suits their needs. If you find yourself in need of support, it is right there and then that your family turns their back on you. They turn a deaf ear to your pleas and a blind eye to your tears. The people surrounding you, putting on the mask of being family, only rub salt on your wounds. These people who once held the same 'blood contract' recognize your existence only when it serves their agendas. These people believe they are better off investing their time elsewhere, where they can reap some benefits at least. Togetherness is a myth when a person hits rock bottom.

I often wonder who needs an enemy when your own family is quick to jump the gun, when they begin pointing fingers and gossiping behind your back. In the same manner, my pain and loss was nothing but a mere means of entertainment for such people to turn into a mockery. They ridiculed my bleeding heart instead of granting me the simplest gesture of condolence. I am only human, and I was incapable of this barter system where you give something in exchange for love and care. Judas betrayed Jesus too; then who am I to expect more from these people?

As a famous Bosnian saying goes, *"Dobro se obucite, vani su hladni ljudi."* It means *"Dress warm, there are cold people outside."* I believe it refers to the kind of cold that fosters loneliness and confusion, making you feel estranged. 'Blood relationship' meant nothing at all – I was sharing genetic code with those who were further from me than even strangers. My intention of finding a home led me further away from the simplest of solace.

I was desperate for a sense of belongingness and purpose. All I wanted to do was fit in somewhere, anywhere to have people surround me even if I did not know them. My desperation led to me becoming a mystery to myself. Yes, I was able to recognize my features each morning in the mirror as I would get dressed for the day. But the person deep behind this skin was a stranger. This new creation and birthing were a result of my grief. My pain pulsed wildly through my body and made me lose control of my thoughts. I began investing my time in the wrong people, hoping to secure happiness from new bonds rather than salvaging the bonds that were always there for me. It seemed easier to start anew than to work on ailing relationships. I shifted my focus to love that was no more than an illusion, to the false hope of countless empty promises by these new strangers calling themselves my friends.

With time, I found my soul aching more than before without understanding how to heal it. This was the price I was paying as I slipped into denial. Had I accepted my loss, perhaps my heart would have been less bedraggled, and I would have been a little less broken. However, here I was unsure of where I belonged. Despite seven billion people being on this planet, I fell at the expanse of emptiness, abandoned from all who I knew and loved with all my heart. All I was left with was dejection.

I began noticing clumps of my hair on the pillow in the mornings. Brushing my hair was worrisome to me, as handfuls of hair would be left on my brush. I avoided brushing my hair as much as I could. In this sadness, I was not the only victim to the brutality of the death of a beloved. Beside me was also the one person who always stood by me in every step of life, my dad. He too, just like me, was a victim, having lost his support system. This elderly man who was beside me was no longer recognizable. He was just a frail man, bent over from the years of storms he had braved one after another. Life was just as ungracious to him as it was to me. We were not rendered any hope or mercy.

This meant that I was losing another important figure in my life - my father. The thought was far crueler than to have lived through nightmares each night. I felt a part of me begin to deteriorate. I was aware and afraid at the same time where this would lead me. I would surely be stranded on a land unknown. However, I did not stop doubting the sincerity and honesty of those around me. My mind was constantly skeptical and cynical, but I craved to be surrounded with assurance and condolence. This tunnel that I was treading in had no light to guide me, deluding my sense of direction.

I learned that these new friends I made were nonexistent, a fragment of my despondent imagination. These people were nothing but a false pretense, a regretful expectation, an unwritten and unspoken verbal contract that would be voided by the lies that erupted from them. Truly, it was this harshest of storms that taught me none of them would be near me when life hit. They selfishly distance themselves when there is nothing more for them. No one wants to burden themselves with the baggage of another. Real situations exposed real friends.

When they no longer have a use for you, they discard you, much like burning out a cigarette. They even step on you as they walk away. I was nothing but a ghost to these people. My circle of *"friends"* became a cage for me and solitary confinement. Death seemed more inviting than this misery. I needed to heal desperately, but it seemed I was getting further from it. The more I thought of filling up my wounds, the more they bled. I was falling endlessly in a bottomless pit, and with each passing second, I prayed to either land or crash.

Instead, each new day, I found myself being my biggest opposition. It was foolish of me to have trusted another to be there for me. It was my dumb hope that people actually cared for me, when all that my pain and I were to them was amusement. It was stupid of me to have been hopeful and looking forward to a miracle that could have halted my mom's death. From there, each time I tried to find myself in the image on the mirror, I found my reflection betraying me. Bit by bit, darkness clutched me tightly in its cold grasp to pull me in the undertow.

Where was it taking me against my will? I knew I did not want to lose myself, but I did not put up a fight to regain control. I hid behind a mask, an accessory I preferred to wear instead of honesty. I started to rely on the convenience of a plastic smile to create the illusion that I was happy, hoping it might come true. Each time, I forced myself to laugh a little louder at things and people who were far from being humorous. This hoax was triumphant in making the people around me believe that my soul was light when in truth it was only hobbling to its death. I became natural in putting up a show.

It instilled a strange sense of pride in me that I was getting the hang of being a successful sham. My intention was to veil my inner turmoil, so one day it would turn into a reality, to fake it until I made it. However, all that it did was break me. Shortly after my mom's death, I noticed the letters and cards stopped coming. The consolation dimmed until it was completely extinguished, abandoning me to find my way out of the darkness. Everyone moved on with their lives, unaware that no matter how hard I tried to move on, I could not.

The darkness engulfed me, terrified me. I learned that these people were only spectators of grief and empathy. Very few friends chose to stick by my side and lend me their hands. These friends prayed for my heart to heal, and stop its anguished churning. In spite of their prayers and wishes, my mind was too paralyzed to even comprehend their help. I began seeing myself as a victim of my loss and started to embrace it, leading me to my damnation. I got three bereavement days from work. Only three days! What could I do in three days? My world had stopped and three days would not be sufficient to put the pieces back together.

And so, instead of taking the opportunity, I turned pessimistic and started scrutinizing the situation. The sun would come up each day, yet my world was no longer illuminated. I became angry, and my explosive anger began to affect my relationships. I could not quite identify what I was angry at, so I misplaced it every chance I got. The more I raged, the worse I felt. I wanted everyone around me to be as miserable as I was. This was possibly the darkest color of my grief. I just wanted to give up and let go, ignoring how it was not good for me to forget how to function.

I stopped trying, blaming the others for not being in my position. I concluded they could never relate to my pain. I became my biggest enemy. My grandmother had a progressive stage of dementia at this time. Her continued questions regarding my stepmother rubbed salt on my already stinging wounds.

"Where is she?" my grandmother would question, with a puzzled look on her face each time someone would come to visit her. Even in her pain, my grandmother was worried about my mom. We began lying to her, saying that she went to the store. It was just too heartbreaking to watch my grandmother learn about my stepmother's death over and over. How can a parent, even if by law, accept that their beloved has left them? My grandmother began to decline,

leaving the rest of us to dwell in another phase of anxiety and distress. Watching my grandmother's health deteriorate drastically became another pill that was bitter and hard to swallow. This trigger of grief recalled all my memories of the first loss to the surface, just when I was trying to shun them completely. The same clouds of gloom hovered above our lives again.

My grandmother was the center point of our family, much like the heart to the body. The thought that we were to lose this crucial member of our family was beyond painful. We needed her to keep all of us functioning; her beats were the only melody in our dull lives. She was an epitome of strength. The sight of her fading was like a stab at my heart. We watched helplessly, as the memories of her life, her heroic antics in WWII, as well as her wisdom began to diminish. The essence of her was dissipating into thin air.

Despite that, however, despite the heart monitor connected to her perpetually, she was just as quick to smile at everyone. Even when her identity was dimming, she was the same sweet woman. This curse of death was draining us all at this point. We were forced to watch another family member leave us. And so shortly after my stepmother's death too. I was not given a chance to recover from one heartache before another leaped to pull me down. My mind replayed the agonizing memories of losing my stepmother. I tried to salvage each memory of my grandmother, trying to tuck it away within the safest corner of my heart and soul for eternity so that I would have something to hold onto and look back on. I began collecting her essence as if it was a souvenir, soaking up all aspects of her presence within me. I wanted to immortalize her, even though a part of me knew she was just a guest in our lives now. And soon, she too left us, leaving me alone. Letting this emptiness stamp its mark on me.

The only difference with this loss was that I learned not to lean on God. Dementia is one of the most painful illnesses to deal with, and I had to watch my grandmother suffer its effects each day. Watching your loved one lose their sense of self is unbearable. I felt as if someone was squeezing my heart in their palm. I began noticing that my grief started with each decline she had. On the 10th of March, 2011, my grandmother, this brave soul, passed away in the ICU at Magic Valley Regional Medical Hospital.

I begged, screamed and pleaded. I prayed silently for my grandmother to stay with me. I hoped endlessly for a miracle to take place even if I had lost faith. She was all I had to cherish, and I wanted her to stay a little longer. I wanted some more time, but I knew that I would never have been able to bid her goodbye and let her soul be free from this world around us. I would have been greedy. Yet I couldn't stop wishing for some more time, to capture her essence for a rainy day.

My grandmother and I

Holidays became difficult in the absence of my mother and grandmother. It was as if the seasons had lost their festivity. These holidays were just as cold as the winters in

Idaho. I tried to induce normalcy back in my life, sitting on my couch and making a list of gifts for the loved ones still with me. But my consciousness had a mind of its own. It became a hindrance. It stopped me from planning anything for my daughter, then just a baby. I felt guilty to be moving on with my life when I had lost the two most important figures in my life. As a mother, it broke me. I failed when I tried to block the horrid memories. As hard it is for anyone to lose their beloved, it's tenfold worse for us refugees. There are so few of us already. Some of our family is back in our hometowns, and others are deceased from the catastrophe of a fatal war. Yet our fate continues to be gruesome.

With this significant loss, it became impossible for me to celebrate, or even feel the merriment of the season. I was numb. My initial gut reaction was to scrap everything and not 'do' vacations or holidays. For the sake of my daughter, I tried to hang the stocking on the fireplace, only to notice the nails that would hold up my grandmother's and stepmother's stockings sticking out like sore thumbs: brutal reminders of our loss. Those barren nails mocked my tragedy. They reminded me of the very memories I wanted to block.

My initial reaction was to cancel my vacations and holidays. I did not want to go through them with the heavy presence of the deceased still lingering. My longing for them, my desire for them to celebrate the holiday with me, it tortured my already berserk mind. My subconscious, therefore, deemed it best not to partake in any festivity. However, because my daughter was still very young, I had to drag my feet against my will, for the sake of the child who wanted to celebrate the occasion. After all, it would have been impossible to make a little child understand why I despised the idea of a holiday now.

She would not have understood why her mother was assailed by the memories of people who were no longer amongst us. Anyway, making her understand would mean I'd have to relive the horrid trauma all over again. Deep within, I knew I should not be selfish. It was natural for my daughter to be ecstatic at the prospect of holidays, just like any child would be. It would have been unfair to her. It made me realize that I should learn to cope with grief better and that I should create coping mechanisms that let me accept life the way it is, where death is inevitable. It is a harsh truth we all will continue to face, but that should not hinder our moving on.

I told myself my stepmother and grandmother would not have wanted me to remain in this state of despair and sorrow for so long. It would hurt them to see me mourning endlessly, missing the opportunity to make newer memories that would be just as precious as theirs. I wanted to move on for my daughter. I had to set an example for her, to show her how to tackle life and all the problems it entails. I also wanted to be a role model for her. But for that, I would first have to learn to cater to my own emotions.

My stepmom's and grandmother's graves

These were no less than a shipwreck, the pieces inaccessible, fueled by memories locked away at the bottom of my heart. My soul was unwilling to help myself recover, so how could I have helped anyone else? Each time I saw the smile on my daughter's face, however, I found my reason to live. My emotions would surge and my mind would decide, *yes, I could cope with this.*

However, as the seconds of the day would tick by, my mind would become numb. Everything was there for me to ponder over. Yet my soul would be in a state of bleak oblivion.

The funny thing about grieving for the loss and memories of a loved one is that it is the ones still living and breathing who suffer throughout this process. It is important to let grief run its course, like the fever that grips our body and goes away in due time after physical care. In the same way, grief needs care in order to run its course, followed by the closure of the heart and mind.

"Grief doesn't have a plot. It isn't smooth. There is no beginning and middle and end."

-Ann Hood

Chapter 5
In My Purgatory I Found Salvation

Death is a certainty for all of us. We are never far from it, only closer every second. One moment we are breathing, and the next we leave behind everything as it is. In a way, we have our whole life to prepare for this moment. We all know this very well. We are not immortals. So why do we find ourselves surprised when we lose a dear one? Why do we become desperate to have a second, a minute, an hour, a day, a lifetime more with them again in our lives?

Death is the center of human experience, as delicate and important as birth is. Death is a re-birth, a re-entry into another world. This doom and inevitable decay of the body becomes the regeneration of the soul. Freeing the soul from the body is essentially what death is all about. It is the separation of a soul and body that spent decades living as one. Each one of us blessed with life will perish, no matter how much we hope, wish, and pray for longer life, whether for ourselves or for those who are dear to us.

Rather than hoping for the soul to depart from the body as peacefully as possible, our emotions aggravate us into an agitating trauma that gnaws away at our sanity. We sacrifice our mental peace to postpone death as if it is possible. Grief makes us question our mortality. We find ourselves musing over how we will meet death when it'll be our turn. Will we meet it with dignity or fear? I don't think anyone can really answer this question until the moment comes near. Death is unpredictable.

We can only guess and make assumptions, like shooting an arrow in the vast sky hoping it will strike something - when it falls, we will get our answer. I am certain that no matter what our beliefs are about life after death, most of us will review our lives - an endless reflection comprising self-doubts and futile consolation. Did we live it well? Did my time on this earth assist others? Or was I confined by selfishness?

Was my impact large enough? Will I be remembered, or did I miss the opportunity to better myself and those around me? We will be left to conclude that we should have prepared ourselves better for our demise. As they say, the hardest situations in life give the biggest lessons. It is true even if we choose to be ignorant, thinking we have time. My losses left my world empty, yet strangely full like a falling star - a pain that is mesmerizingly tragic. Each grief triggered another, a domino effect. The havoc that resonates within our fumbling soul makes us look around frantically in hopes of spotting light. It is then, in the darkness, that we begin to see the stars if we choose to look up. We search for the most trivial of glistening pinpricks in the hopes of it rekindling our dim sorrows. But no matter how hard I wish to have all the things and people I lost in my life back, it will not happen. The time that is gone is time lost. This is why they say that time is a gift to us. However, more than often we take this gift for granted, only to cry later.

My lessons from grief will last me a lifetime. All these losses left me with so many lessons - to look at life from a different perspective and bask in its glory while embracing its imperfection. My stepmother's death gave my life an opportunity to live my life in a better and wiser way. I used to run away from grief as if I was running from a mortal enemy. I never knew how strong I was, that I could carry a burden far more wearisome than I had. Her death gifted me the ability to recognize the value of a moment and cherish it when it is gone until my last breath.

Right now, as you are reading this, this moment will never come back. We will never have a *now* again. Accept this moment that you are given, even if you feel heartache or rejoice. One day you will look back at this day and wish to have lived it a little better. For myself, today I choose to live life like this. Each moment is valuable. I would not have learned had I not suffered from losses, irrecoverable and inevitable.

My grief gave me a more tender heart and an empathetic soul. It gave me an opportunity to relate to those around me. It gave me the chance to speak out about my grief, about my love, and my loss. It rejuvenated my faith in moving on, rather than to freeze in pain. Not doing anything about the pain would mean I was stuck in quicksand, which over time, could have swallowed me whole.

My mother's death, along with all of the other losses I survived awakened my spirituality, transcending my ego into the collective consciousness. It was the realization of my existence in relation to humanity and the world around me. This consciousness pulled me out of the *'me'* mentality and opened my eyes up to see myself and my life in relation to those around me. I am not the only one who has encountered grief; others have too. We are all caught up in a whirlwind of emotions that we greedily take from others, leaving them depleted. We all grieve over things in life. No one of us has immunity to any kind of loss. One might have wealth, health, or the greatest joy of a family. But in any case, no one us gets the whole cake. We grieve over the loss of jobs, loss of relationships, loss of things, and loss of people. Losses are the harsh reality of our life that we cannot avoid at any cost. We encounter grief frequently in life, so I choose to focus on the lessons from these losses. I choose to push past *me* into the understanding and acceptance that I will continue to lose things. It is my perception of these losses that will pull me out of my grief or dig me deeper into it. All that is within my control is to let my loss make me either stronger or weaker.

Once I instilled within my mind the concept of having the liberty to make such a decision, I began to shed my grief. Me, the person who was lost in grief for ten years. The person who I no longer know and need to discover again. Who I was in the past transcended into a survivor, thanks to the birthing that came out of loss. I needed to rediscover the survivor in me so that I would continue to grow than uproot my opportunities. As humans, we are continuously evolving. If I too wished to evolve, I would naturally have to go through a trauma and overcome the obstacles to nurture and move on. At the age of forty, a person is still dreaming of seamless momentums, but do not have anything to trigger. You feel that you are too old to do so. I find myself learning how to be content with my accomplishments and missed opportunities. We are never too old to learn. Each day brings forth new scenarios and challenges from which we can learn.

Age is not reason enough for us to defy our potential for achievements. It is just a fictional chain that holds us down. I resisted this fictional chain to set myself free, to learn, grow, and fill my glum sky with colors for myself and for all those around me. This is my opportunity, and my setbacks have equipped me with enough wisdom to alleviate my sufferings as well as of those who surround me.

The undying love of my father

In my grief, I thought God had abandoned me. However, I came to learn that it was not so. This anguish taught me to face myself. In essence, I found God through this. I feel like this is the hardest task for some of us. For some people, it comes easy. Others have to struggle to figure out who God is, the hard way. Through my trials and tribulations, I learned how to stare at my reflection rather than to ignore it. Ignorance is not always bliss.

I believe the hardest of all tasks we can do as humans is to climb out of the abyss of despair, to carry our emotional baggage on our shoulders, and strive forward. Life becomes a journey that leaves our soles bleeding with each step, and yet we fight the resistance. By watching my patients through hospice, I learned this is what we do when we are preparing to die. Face ourselves - a task that by all definitions is very humbling. To face all the things that are ugly about me. To face all the things that are honest and beautiful too.

Grief is an ongoing process without clear stages or end. It is a never-ending process. It does not disappear. It changes and evolves, but it remains. Although it becomes less intense, we forever grieve over things that we lose. However, belief and spirituality give us an opportunity to remember that there will be a time where we will get to meet our loved ones again. Hence, instead of counseling people to help them cope better with their sorrow, I teach people there are no clear stages of grief each of them will face. The counseling field teaches that there are five stages of a repetitive pattern for every person. I found out that the counseling field had it all wrong. My belief and experiences gave me a different lens to examine grief. There are no particular stages of grief. Stages depict a routine, some kind of a chronological order that makes us assume we will have to go through each stage before we can heal in a fixed sequence.

They are not stages. They are emotional reactions .The

stages of grief that are taught to most clients in the counseling field are not stages, but emotional reactions to loss. When I worked with clients in counseling, I referenced a person's recovery process of grief and not stages of grief. I am well-versed in the mental health and the grief stages. So instead of teaching about this pattern that has been devised like an imaginary tool, we need to teach building resilience to grief. If I accept the concept of stages, that means there is an unspoken expectation that I progress through them. However, what if I do not encounter them all in my grief? The concept of stages insinuates that I need to move through these stages in some order.

If I do not, then something is wrong with me. This is the biggest contradiction in itself. Stages do not exist, recovery from grief does. We all are unique. Our sorrow and pain are different from one another. Then, how can we all have the same solution? If one key cannot open all locks, then why do we assume these stages tend to all broken hearts? I recall that about 10 years ago, I sat in a grief counseling session with a client. This person was going through the pain of having lost her son. The woman kept repeating that she had been trying to get through the anger stage of grief for the past two years.

She believed she was stuck in a stage, as if life was a game. Moreover, her emphasis that she was not able to move past her anger flicked on the realization: somehow, my counseling had failed. That was my moment of clarity - what I was teaching was not effective. What I learned in school was not effective. The anger that my client was experiencing was damaging relationships around her.

Yet, her certainty allowed her to think that because it was a stage of grief, it would pass. She then found herself wondering what was wrong with her when this stage did not pass. This belief of being damaged and stuck in her grief immobilized her and made her believe that she could not get through it. Her feeling of being stuck paralyzed her. Her belief that she had to get through the stage immobilized her for two years. To see her be stuck in the misery caused my heart to ache, and I was unable to find a remedy for her within any textbook. No theory, no thesis could ease this concept of hers that she was stuck in.

So, what we need to teach clients is not stages, but to help them build resilience in order to move on. Focus on resilience. The concept of stages of grief was developed initially as stages of death and then spread like a virus to the counseling field. What does it mean to go through stages? It means that you need to jump through them in some type of order when in truth grief has no order. The concept of stages gives people the idea that they have to enter them, and if they do not, then they are not grieving correctly. These stages are nothing but an idle concept.

The only thing that exists is resilience and recovery. You have to learn how to be resilient to your pain. Only then will you be able to recover from it. It is not an easy task to be resilient, especially if you lose a very dear person. It is excruciatingly agonizing and can even take up to years. However, we need to know that there is nothing wrong with taking time. One person's strength is not the same as another's. We grieve based on how close we were to the person that we lost, our cultural teachings, our family rituals, and our knowledge. Denial, anger, bargaining, depression, and acceptance are not stages of grief but our emotional reaction to it. We do not necessarily have to experience all of them to begin adjusting to life.

We believe everything we see on the virtual world that interlinks us all. We live in a world where major life events are publicized on social media. This fantasy world shows an unrealistic vision of our lives. False friendships have contributed to distancing us further from social interactions. Our world is surrounded by social media interactions that are becoming more important than real-life interactions. We, as humans, are beginning to lose our humanity.

I fear we will soon forget the human touch and hug, as they are replaced with all the emojis and reactions on our social media. However, these imaginary gestures cannot compensate for the physical interaction and the presence of a person next to you. We are beginning to lose the ability to empathize with and support those around us. We are beginning to see what benefit we can get from one another as opposed to the ability to exist in relationships with an open heart.

When we look at Facebook or Instagram, we get to know that this is a deluded depiction of a flawless life. We promote the dinner we had with our loved ones. We paint a picture of this perfection when we are farthest from that. In truth, we are slowly putting an end to physical human interaction. Even though social media has its benefits, allowing you to be in touch with people who do not live near you, we are starting to rely on it even to give support upon a close one's demise! We tend to leave messages on their Facebook page.

If we are extending our condolence via social media, would it not be the same as praying for them from afar when they need our presence the most? We distance ourselves unknowingly from one another. However, condolences on social media do not necessarily leave a person feeling supported in their grief. It does nothing. Words without action are desolate. What would support a grieving person is perhaps a hug, or someone sitting next to them. A human touch and being able to look at someone in close proximity can do wonders. It is crucial to express what you feel for a person, not through social media but through genuine human interaction.

Grief in the context of social media extends to posting our feelings about the loss of the deceased. We post on our loved one's social media pages through continued updates, noting things we are thinking and reflecting our progress in grief for others to witness. In a way, we create virtual cemeteries to immortalize our loved ones and, from time to time, post on their page as a way of communicating our messages to them.

We live in a society where the most common type of grief is a virtual one. Even when it comes to support, we are virtually consoled. Does this leave a person feeling as if they are supported in their grief? No. Society has changed in this sense, and I must say I suffered my losses early on before my realization of social media grief. I am glad for this.

One of the worst advice I have heard and read regarding consoling someone is to give time, as time is the best of healers. They say that time heals all wounds. What a dangerously bogus thought it is! Give it some time, people say. Time on its own does nothing. So if I sit in my misery and wait for time to pass, that will not heal me. If after a certain time, my grief stays unchanged, then I will wonder what is happening with me - why is my heart not mended yet? The answer is that I did nothing to mend my broken heart. Time has the magical power we have to obtain and work with. But it is not a charm that will fill our wounds. It is what we do with what time we have that will bring about resilience and relief. It is my effort that brings about a change. It is what I do in my grief that leads me to heal. For the first time, I felt the beginning of my healing deep within my soul. I began stitching my wounds. I learned that even amidst the darkness, there was a desire we all possessed to survive the things we thought we could not. Through service to others, I learned that even in the darkest moments of our life, the sun would shine if we allowed it to. I learned that we all struggle with grief at some point and that I am not the only one. We are all a little broken, and everyone needs some healing in their life. It is the crack within our heart that reflects how nothing is meant to be perfect.

That moment when I was able to cater to someone else was when I felt the most alive. It is when I do something, not for myself, but for someone else. That's what matters. It allows me to feel connected with humans. It allows me to interact and help. It allows me to build on the experiences that I will want to remember when I die. Just like when our neighbor gave us those drumsticks – I can never forget what it felt like to have him help us when my family and I were. I essentially do that for people when I have the means. I have had numerous homeless people live with me in my home until they get back on their feet. It is my way of giving back. It is something that was given to me when I was homeless, and now I get to give back. I am fortunate now that I do have a roof over my head, and I love to help people get back on their feet. I can relate to their pain, yet I aspire to do more than that.

Even though war and the loss of my home were painful, it led me to discover human beings or angels on this earth like Nediljko. Now who am I to forget that today, when I have enough food and resources, I need to do the same for someone else? We all can do more of that. We all can help others a little bit more. We get wrapped up in our lives and explain away why someone is standing on the corner of the street, instead of walking over to them and asking if they are all right.

My art

I feel like we all can do a little something for someone.

The things I do for others I will remember for the rest of my life. But the things I do for myself become forgotten a year from now. So those are the things that make me feel alive and purposeful. We all, in a sense, have a responsibility to uphold one another, uplift one another, and stand tall.

Each of us walking on this earth is not doing so in vain. We all can do something for someone, even if it is opening a door. During the process of writing this book, I lost another person - a best friend. Vesna passed away from cancer. A month after I commenced this reflective memoir of mine, my friend left this world. This was another loss in my life. However, this time this loss did not trigger similar emotions. This time it had an adverse implication. I am different now, and so my ability to perceive this loss today is different than when I lost my mother and grandmother. I began speaking about my grief to anyone who would listen. However, most people are uncomfortable when it comes to grief. I found it hard to find someone willing to partake in the cup of my grief. Hard to find, but there are little gems that are willing to grieve alongside you. I get the privilege of doing that with my job as a hospice medical social worker.

What a privilege it is to simply exist in the moment with someone grief-stricken - to get to be a part of someone's healing and hear how strong they have been even in moments of isolation and woe! By inducing these changes, my perception of grief changed. I began to talk about my loss - the dark mass of grief that was growing bigger within me like a black hole. As I began talking about my loss, this black hole started to decrease in size. This grief started to dissipate. I realized the power it had over me was waning. I chose to hug my grief and sit with it, spend time in that pain and misery, and just grieve.

I allowed myself to cry and have a crappy day. And when I did that, I started noticing that the crappy days were decreasing, though I still had them. I normalized them. It is OK to have a crappy day when we lose someone. I discovered that genuine human concern is powerful. It was one of these antidotes that I needed to pull out of grief. I learned a lot of things during that period. I learned that it is an honor to hold the hand of someone who is entering the last moments of their life. I learned that our presence alone is powerful. Most people do not need to hear anything specific.

They just want to know that you are there with them, present at the moment, and that they are not alone in their last moments. The funny thing is, at one point, I was the one who needed help and reassurance. But things changed after I changed. I was no longer a victim then. I was rather a survivor. The moment I identified myself as a survivor, I started seeing things that justified my perception of myself. It is our perception that matters the most. It is our ability to conceive things positively for them to have an impact. In a transition such as this, it is important to have someone who understands you – every step of the way.

To my surprise, I learned that not everyone would be there when you need them. And in the darkest of days, the most surprising people come to be your guiding light. The ones who I had thought were going to stay with me through thick and thin were nowhere in sight. Through my losses, I lost friendships. To a grief-stricken person, this is like a knife slicing an already open wound. People I truly would have given my life for abandoned me in my misery.

The betrayal that comes from such friendship is a wound that may never heal. Even if it does at some point, it leaves behind a scar, a question without an answer, an abandonment that will never find ease. Not everyone stayed in my life, no matter how much I loved them or how much I wanted them. Not everyone was able to console a grief-stricken person either.

These people started to look at me quizzically each time they saw my face doused in sorrow. Their silence sought permission to go. I pictured myself waving my hand in approval, *"Go!"* I motioned to others, and they did with no hesitation. They did not want to be there anyway, so why should I have held them? *"Go before you become witness to my weakness."* Although life has given me one too many reasons to cry, I would be a much different person if I hadn't faced the harshest of storms. This left me capable of being there for other aching souls. My child, my family, and my friends will never have to wonder where to go for a hug, for support, and for love. I choose to open my arms as wide as I can and welcome them in their time of need. I sit with them in their time of misfortune. I vowed to be everything I needed and lacked in my grief. So whether those around you pull back during your loss, or lend a shoulder to you to cry on, remember that you are not alone. Reach people and offer love, as love is the very substance of our human existence. Be kind and compassionate to another. It is the most valuable gift we can offer to another dejected person.

We spend most of our lives chasing things of value - a bigger house, a bigger paycheck, a better car, etc. Our expectations of presents are no less materialistic either. We overlook the fact that these materialistic things provide us with a temporary sentient of likeness. Every time we receive a gift, we cherish it until our last breath. Time, friendship, and love are what's valuable and leave behind an everlasting imprint. I learned that time is the greatest value we have. Time with our loved ones is a priceless commodity that cannot be bought and cannot be sold either.

It is an hourglass that continues to pour out until the last grain of sand falls out. It is of value – alas that it perishes, just like we all will. It does not bind us. The grief shackles of my misery began loosening up the moment I was ready to release them. They were only holding me back because I made the decision to confine myself in the echoes of dread. I was now ready to start separating myself from my grief, to liberate myself from the prison I was captured in. I only started healing when my perception and understanding of loss began changing, much like seasons change from one to another.

I chose to change my attitude about what happened to me. To begin seeing myself as a survivor instead of a victim. I began realizing that I was very much immobilized by the grief of my perception regarding loss - my personal experience of these losses. If I focused on misery, then all I could see around were things that justified it. If I focused on healing, I began associating things around me that gave me opportunities to heal. By the very act of recognizing the loss, you begin the long journey to recovery. I found solace in the blessings I started to count instead of weeping over my misfortune.

To others, I represented just another person who experienced a loss. To myself, I was in the midst of a debilitating, life-changing hell. Just like any other unpleasant experiences, we tend to focus on running away, shielding ourselves and firing back if possible. Instead of opening up our hearts, we seek comfort in a hideout. It is better not to know rather than to anticipate something, only for it to fail on us. We, ourselves, limit our ability to accept rejection, setbacks, and losses.

What I found helpful was learning how to stand my ground in the midst of this storm. Even though it felt like I would not survive or it might kill me, I began standing up. I began to realize that in order to get through grief, I needed to stop allowing myself to be degraded by the almost abusive relationship I had developed with my grief.

Deep within, I always knew I had the power to stop the poison of sorrow from spreading within me, a poison that harbored the power to seize my life. I just had to muster up the courage and will myself to do so. My voyage out of grief began with small steps. I stopped running from the pain of this, but began instead to immerse myself in it. To fight the demon of suffering, I first had to understand it and all of its wicked trickery. This crippling, debilitating pain was showing me that I was very much alive. So instead of being forced to categorize myself under the stages of grief and marginalize my whole existence, I began showing the kindness toward myself that I was expecting from others. This meant to stand my ground in the face of strong emotional reactions to grief. It felt as if I was going to battle, but I made a decision deep within myself - I was tired of running from grief and being a victim in its hand. I was not a victim to it. I was not going to let it suffocate me. I was a survivor.

I began hugging grief as if I was hugging a best friend and embraced every moment of it, no matter how painful it was. After all, I was not only grieving the loss of my mother, but all the losses I had experienced up until this point. It was a timely process that initially discouraged me – I was scared of not bearing the pain. I had to show myself the courage to pick myself back up and continue this walk of life one step at a time.

Grief also taught me patience. They say patience is of virtue. If you master patience, you regain the steering wheel of your life. From there, you can navigate your life in any direction. Patience with the time that it was taking me to process my loss taught me that grief cannot be rushed. It is processed in our own way with the skills we have to deal with it. We just have to dig deep within ourselves to exploit our potential for the betterment of our soul. For some, the duration of grief is longer than for others. The duration itself is individualized. No two people are alike; then why should their life and all it entails be? Grief is not a mundane routine. It is a remarkable norm.

The best thing you can do is take one second at a time than to live through the whole phase with the blink of an eye.

Our habit of rushing things is the major reason why we fall weak at the hands of grief. As hard it is to go through suffering, we cannot undo it. The only remedy is to live through it much against our desire. The ache and pain are unfathomable, but we deceive our mind with lies about finding an instant cure. In this society, we are accustomed to treating any type of discomfort as soon as it occurs.

From an early age, we are taught that pain is bad. So when we feel discomfort, we are immediately offered *a fix*. That fix comes mostly in forms of pills. Take a pill and all will be healed. In truth, this theory only works like a Band-Aid. Put this band-aid on, and it will hold until someone or something rips it off. At that point, we go back to square one. This way of numbing is no different than the way an alcoholic/drug addict numbs their pain. Now I do recognize that some of us may need medication, but do not allow it to be the only way to heal from grief. It is what you do in grief that brings healing. Medications can help, but medications alone do not fix it. Trust your own self rather than a chemical substance or another person. People and medicines have a temporary effect that wears off, expanding the hollowness. Just as our body heals itself when we have a cut, so does our psyche if we allow it to when we begin focusing on resilience and not debilitation. When I began changing the way I was thinking of my pain, healing began to occur.

Pain is not bad. Emotional pain will not kill me unless I allow it to. It is unbearable and we all go through varying forms and intensity of grief, but we can overcome it. We have that potential. We are unwilling to look for a solution within ourselves. The reason can be different, be it fear of losing more or encountering a calamity far worse. But by not facing our misery, we become our own destruction. Pain is bad, yet it has the potential to make us stronger and move on.

Adopt certain measures to complement your journey through the barren desert of grief and into the lush oasis of self-healing. One such measure is having daily rituals. These bring on resilience. It forces us to do something with our grief. It requires action. It brings on reconciliation of our misfortune. Simply doing something forces us to hope that things can improve. Our life offers varying phases of bliss and tranquility, sadness and despair. But each phase is not lasting. Like seasons, our lives change. Until that change, we have to force ourselves to seek even a grain sized antidote.

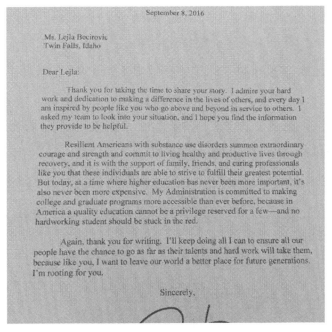

September 8, 2016

Ms. Lejla Becirovic
Twin Falls, Idaho

Dear Lejla:

Thank you for taking the time to share your story. I admire your hard work and dedication to making a difference in the lives of others, and every day I am inspired by people like you who go above and beyond in service to others. I asked my team to look into your situation, and I hope you find the information they provide to be helpful.

Resilient Americans with substance use disorders summon extraordinary courage and strength and commit to living healthy and productive lives through recovery, and it is with the support of family, friends, and caring professionals like you that these individuals are able to strive to fulfill their greatest potential. But today, at a time where higher education has never been more important, it's also never been more expensive. My Administration is committed to making college and graduate programs more accessible than ever before, because in America a quality education cannot be a privilege reserved for a few—and no hardworking student should be stuck in the red.

Again, thank you for writing. I'll keep doing all I can to ensure all our people have the chance to go as far as their talents and hard work will take them, because like you, I want to leave our world a better place for future generations. I'm rooting for you.

Sincerely,

First of 2 letters received from the President of the United States

We live in a society where there is significance placed on nutrition. Resilience to grief cannot be denied when it comes to nutrition. Have you ever dieted before? The majority of people have. If you have, then I am sure you know the feeling when you have been dieting for some time. At one point, you begin to notice that you are starting to feel better. Resilience to grief is imperative in terms of nutrition. If my psyche is not well, and on top of that my body is not well, then I am in a way magnifying my discomfort. But if I choose to feed my body well during the times my psyche is struggling, it will at least give me a boost in energy, which is much needed when you find yourself immersed in grief. Lack of nutrition fosters illness, and illness and grief together are not the right combination.

Through healing, we begin mending our broken pieces. We humans, through simple experience on this earth, begin learning how to stand strong during difficult situations. Our lives teach us that standing strong is easy when life is okay, but standing strong during challenges allows us to get stronger. Grief is hard enough. Suffering is hard enough. Yet most of us choose to suffer in silence, with masks on our faces, pretending that life is good. Silent grief is the hardest. The kind that brings us to our knees when we are alone. Those of us who grieve in silence pay a high price for companionship. We are unable to differentiate between sincerity and lies when our eyes are misty and our hearts are vacant. Having to go through the pain that no one else can understand pushes us deeper into the pit of melancholy.

People around us smile and laugh while we sit and cry alone. Things start to paint a picture of sorrow, leaving us to envy the happiness of others. We forget that there was once a time when we too were merry and the other was in a phase of distress.

We have become vain and selfish in our society. The media has played such a huge part in this area to discourage our empathy and compassion. The desire for a certain body type or certain status spreads easily, when kindness and humanity should be promoted widely. We have been immersed in a Kardashian-like world. But what about the heart? What about compassion? What about empathy for the human person? What about genuine and unconditional love for one another? What about support in time of need? Supporting a grief-stricken person does not mean repeating some wise-sounding phrases you think will change someone's life.

Supporting a grief-stricken person means simply existing in the moment with them so they are not alone, letting them know they are not alone, and checking on them despite the fake smiles on their face. During the loss of my best friend Vesna, out of all of the friends I have had, three people reached out to me. Only three remained in the time of need. I do not mean reaching in terms of condolence. I mean reaching continuously through the loss. Some came over and just sat with me.

That was all I needed. Just the presence of someone who cared enough to just sit there and exist in grief with me. They took time out of their day to bring a bag full of teas that would help me settle down and sleep. A few gems in my life of genuine friendship and concern. Now that I reflect on my anguish, it is not the words they said or the tea they brought along, but their faces full of concern for me that leaves me remembering them. That eased my heart's yearning of belongingness.

I met one of these gems in the counseling field as she was doing her internship with me. Through her empathy, this person significantly contributed to my rise. She was a strong clinician in this field and her skills outshined others'. She reached out many times not to say anything in particular, but to simply be there. Texts like this would let me know she loved and cared.

"Hey love, I am here just want you to know that you

have been on my mind all day today. We don't see each other nearly enough, but you have a special place in my heart. I am so sorry for all the pain you've gone through and have been going through. Let me know how I can be a little sliver of sunshine in this dark time."

We are taught to chase things of value, rather than to reach out to each another without any motive or agenda. We are living in a world where everyone needs someone, but everyone is immersed in their own ego to notice other's suffering. We only think of ourselves. Not once do we stop and think - does the other person need anything? Are they fine or are they breaking? But why should we burden ourselves with the suffering of another?

We have to tend to our own desires even if they come at the cost of leaving someone drained of love. We only indulge in the inheritance of happiness. What about service to others with no expectation of anything in return? We have become desensitized to human interaction and in this, we are losing our humanity. My few friends who stood by me were not looking for anything in return. Not because I did not have much to give, but because a simple human interaction to a grief-stricken person means the world. This one-sided friendship, as I had nothing to give in return, continues with random coffee dates where no judgment is passed, and we simply exist together in the moment. Their ability to look past the unanswered texts and promises that I would call them back shows understanding. Understanding that in grief we say and do things that some may misinterpret and take personally.

To a grief-stricken person, these behaviors of inconsistency may go unnoticed. So if you have a friend who has encountered grief, do not walk away, but approach them with understanding. Walking away in such sensitive time fosters abandonment and magnifies grief. Practice compassion, forgiveness, and understanding. The friends who offered support were like a reservoir of antidotes that pushed me away from my reclusiveness.

They say if death is expected, which in my mother's case it was, then it gives you time to prepare. This is absurd. No matter what the circumstances, our initial reaction to death is visceral. How do we prepare for something whose effect we have no idea about, or what our reaction to it will be? How can one even think of losing a parental figure, especially when they had been your greatest supporter and your sincerest critic just to make you a better person? We do not prepare. I could never have prepared even when I saw my mother and grandmother's health worsen right before my eyes. Be it denial or unwillingness to accept the bitter reality, I would never have stopped hoping for a miracle that would have healed them. Like a spell that could have bewitched their illness away.

We grasp every ounce of resilience, which is hard. Even though I thought that a miracle would happen with my mom, somewhere in me I knew exactly what was happening. Even though I knew, her death still hit me like a train, leaving me blown away with how it felt. There was no way to prepare for something I had no clue about.

In the counseling field, I have seen clinicians focus on preparing clients in some way to encounter situations that might be difficult for them to face, instead of building resilience so that no matter what happens in life we have ample amount of skills we can use. There is no way to prepare for something that we have not yet encountered. Even if we have gone through the death of a close one, we can never prepare ourselves for the death of another. We cannot deprive ourselves of hope for a better outcome. We should only enhance our ability to accept each adversity and know we could not have changed the course and time of someone's death. I encounter grief differently each time I greet in anew, as I am different in the moments I encounter it. We continue to evolve and change, and our perception naturally changes with that.

Through my loss, I discovered life. In my purgatory, I encountered salvation. I am not a victim of grief but a survivor of it. I am what I chose to become from this and not what happened to me. I discovered a more active way of participating in my grief and my life. I learned to exist in each moment mindfully, a moment that passes quickly and that leaves me with a decision of how I chose to utilize it.

The color of my grief changed from the deepest darkest pit to the hope that I could survive too. My misery did not go unnoticed, but it evolved into something that could save not only me but also others. Opening our eyes during grief may just be one of the hardest things to do. Seeing the world for what it is can be painful. Adjusting to the world without our loved ones is difficult. Remember that there is only one of you, the perfect creation placed on this planet to have a human experience. There is no one like you. No one has the same fingerprints or sense of humor quite like you. No one experiences the world the same way you do. So don't lose the sense of hope in your grief. Welcome help from others and recognize those gems in your life that are willing to grieve alongside you. Treasure the people who are there in your times of hardship. You will survive, even though you may have moments that make you question even your survival. Your mind will break apart your better judgment, telling you it is easier said than done. It is definitely easier said than done, but it does not mean it is impossible.

Audrey Hepburn said: *"Nothing is impossible. Even the word says I'm possible."*

You, the very result of the love of thousands of ancestors, are here to immerse yourself in human experience. You can move mountains if you make that your aspiration. So live in the moment and allow yourself to capture all of the beautiful things that happen in your life. Bathe in the warm sun rays and bask in the beams of the radiant moon when you can. So when a rainy day comes, you could fetch moments of happiness from your memories. Allow yourself to capture all of the difficult things that have happened as well. You have already survived, as you are reading these words. So rediscover a survivor in you.

You are a survivor. You are beautiful. You are loved. You are enough.

My beautiful daughter, my guiding light

I dedicate this book to all of you. You, who have grieved in silence for fear of being judged. You, who have grieved alone as others ran away from you the moment you had nothing to offer. You, who debated on giving up, yet are sitting wherever you are reading these words. You the imperfect, the fallen one. We all frequently fall in life and then rise. You are a survivor. A beautiful creation. Life is not about perfection. It is about getting up when we fall. It is about embracing ourselves, no matter what imperfections we have. In turn, we become better and stronger together.

Life is imperfect, just like people are. Embrace the flaws and let them flow like an endless stream. Learn from the flow of nature that everything will go on. Even the water goes above the rough surface of corals and reef, yet it flows to join the ocean majestically. Even that ocean is bottomless, yet it allows for life to flourish. Your life too will flourish. There will be times when you will suffocate on the ever-growing lump in your throat. There will be times when either the tears will flow profusely or your eyes will run dry.

There will be days that will drive you to the brink of giving up. There will be days when your heart will be numb to pain. At every step, in every moment of your life, you will be alone. We need to accept that people, no matter how much we love them, will leave us one day. Nothing can prepare us for their demise, nor can we deny it. But if you wish for your heart to fly once more, you will have to go through the prickling fence of life that will tether your skin. As you emerge on the other side, the scars will heal, letting you breathe once more.

"We're born alone, we live alone, and we die alone. Only through our love and friendship can we create the illusion for the moment that we're not alone."

-Orson Welles

Chapter 6
I Rise

As a child, not only did I encounter war, grief, hunger, and homelessness, but I had also been a victim of mental abuse. Looking back at that particular phase of my life still causes my heart to tremble, and because of this, I find myself unable to reflect on it. I will save memories of this for another book and for another rainy day, where I will be able to face the horrid memories headstrong instead of quivering and falling back into the abyss of darkness that once plagued my heart, mind, and soul. I will face the abusive memories for when my heart will be ready to heal from all of the bruises.

For now, I only tread along the memory lane of setbacks and losses that humbled me amidst the process of recovery. Healing does not come as easily as people think. It is a task easier said than done. To heal means to relive each and every single memory that has scarred you and yes, I will relive those moments. Alternatively, I feel relieved to have gone through some of the harshest of storms as they have shaped me to be the human I am now. My life experiences have shaped the person I am today. Having cried endlessly,

I now try to wipe away other tear-stained cheeks, and be there to comfort another for I know what it is like to feel all alone, terrified, and scared. I know how excruciatingly painful it is for a person to be a victim of loneliness when they are going through a dilemma. Had it not been the war, then I would never have stumbled across Nediljko, a person who showed us that we were still humans even if we were immersed mercilessly in our personal hell, in the deepest of agonizing flames, burning only for our existence to be diminished baselessly. Had it not been for the monstrosity of others that forced us to flee our home and our sanctuary, I would never have believed in second chances and angels.

Had it not been the goodwill of Nediljko, I would have only remembered my loss, rather than work on rebuilding life from scratch as many times as needed. Angels exist in the guise of humans, like Nediljko, who sheltered us when others only wanted to torch us and relish in our screams. Had it not been the savagery of this world, I would never have been a witness to Nediljko's unprejudiced love and compassion. Not everyone has a deranged mind that wishes to inflict pain on another human being. Some of us mourn at the loss of another, and other hearts ache too in our grief. As a result of this, today I have housed homeless people.

Because I know what it is like to sleep in fear, then waking up and scurrying in search of another roof for shelter. The fear gnaws at the heart and silent tears are shed, yet the homeless person has to put on a brave front in the hopes of deluding their fears even as they create the illusion of hope for those with them. Having gone through this, I simply cannot bear watching another soul go through this dreadful feeling.

My art

Who am I to turn a blind eye to other's misfortune when I myself have encountered hunger and homelessness? Every time I hear or watch someone else go through such sorrow, I envision myself in that person's shoes. Thoughts flash through me then, of when I was that girl who watched other privileged people just pass me by, mocking my misery. I question myself, if I want to be that person capable enough of easing the pain of another, or if I want to numb my heart and go on with my life. I get my answer when my heart beats erratically, reminding me of how I had felt – dejected and humiliated and hopeless. No one should have to go through that, regardless of their race and language. Watching Nediljko render his aid to us made me want to be like him, aim to be like the wonderful person that he was.

No matter what trauma we have encountered in our lives, most of us have that one person who believes in us. That one person who, against all other odds, has influenced us to want to be more like them. In case we do not have them, it should give us all the more reason to be that person for another. Nediljko's aura of simplicity captivated me, making me want to feel as light-spirited as him. I did not want to be weighed down by these chains of misery, which weighed me down despite my having not committed any crime. I too, after all, was punished along with many others. However, Nediljko salvaged my family, for which I would forever be grateful to him.

He showed me that I can always tug on these chains to climb out of the prison that life will continue to place me in. I wanted to be him. I wanted to be this majestic tree that I perceived Nediljko to be, and radiate my shelter over others. A shadow of protection and tranquility that anyone can seek. I wanted to cast a shadow under which any child could prance about freely, rather than spend their childhood frightened about their tomorrow. I cannot change the world, but I can make small changes in others' lives every day, and so start a movement to change the world. I will never forget this priceless lesson he taught me. He sparked this flame of hope and belief within me, and it still resonates in my mind.

His simple belief led me to take charge of my life, and I want to reciprocate his generosity for others. Nediljko is my hero. He saved me from slipping into oblivion without any selfish motive. I want to instill this virtue once more. Maybe, that will inspire another to continue with this wave of kindness and positivity. The little girl whom he saved now wishes to save another child, another parent, and another friend. This kindness is essential to the existence of mankind, and yet we fail to comprehend the gravity of this situation. Without kindness and love, we are all doomed.

Hatred is just a bitter poison that spreads endlessly, but there is an antidote to it. One that Nediljko provided me with, and I savor the taste of it to this date. Now I want to extend this remedy of kindness to brighten other lives as well. A child of war, of homelessness, and of abuse rose out of the ashes of Bosnia into a woman who is living a life of relative peace today. However, the trauma of war still surfaces within me from time to time. The memories and the nights I spend in fear still haunt me. No matter how hard I try, I can never shun my past - the ghost of our past does keep jumping right back up.

Despite this and the nightmares imprinted on my mind, I continue to heal. Closing my eyes, I take in a sharp breath and breathe out to release the knots forming in my stomach – the manifestation of my anxiety. The time that is gone cannot be worked on, but I can make the most of my present for it to shelter the future. Thus, in the hopes of helping someone else, I help myself in turn. I continue to speak and educate others regarding children who are victims of war, PTSD, grief, and loss. Yes, people are aware of the sufferings of others, but being a victim who outlived the odds, I sketch out the possibility of how a little help can go a long way.

This is how I seek my own redemption. My healing comes from helping others. I never received the much-needed satisfaction when I relied on other measures, but when someone else smiled because of me. When I became the reason behind another person's smile, that became my guiding light. I realized people were the ones who had the power to shed light on my moments of despair. Ever since then, I cherish every opportunity to speak of my life so I can impact others. I found I reflected strength for others to be inspired by. I am a human being interconnected with others, and I have the desire to help.

My grief taught me to love deeply before I lose it, so I have memories to savor when life hands me lemons. I have learned that to be remembered, I need to create moments in others' lives that are worth remembering. I need to spark happiness in the heart of another when I can. For this, I am truly blessed in my life to work in the hospice field. I get to do that here by showing that a loss may be inevitable, but it is within our hands to make the most of the last moments. The only thing that can come slightly close to compensating for the missing presence of their loved ones will be the memories filled with smiles and laughter they make now.

Today, I create hand molds with my patients and their loved ones – a unique sculpture of their hands that has forever captured a moment in time for our patient and their loved ones. A moment in time that will pass very quickly for all of us, yet will serve as a reminder of blissful memories. A rainbow only comes after a rainstorm. Happiness prevails after sorrows. And this comes from the will of finding something more. Through my hell, I found God. I was provoked to find a cure to the demons that haunted me. I found faith in the darkest moments.

Desperation pushed me to turn to him. Without those moments, I would still be lost on this earth, unsure how to evolve my spirituality. I was never the one to believe in religion as I have mentioned in the previous chapters. However, when my nightmares started to paralyze my sanity, I knew I had to denounce secularism.

As humans, I feel we are taught first to focus on evolving physically as babies - learning to crawl, then walk, then run. Then adolescence and young adulthood are spent on mental evolution through school, learning and diverging into a career. It is not until late adulthood that we begin searching more for spiritual evolution. Ever since our births, we are thrown into the hustle and bustle of life. It is a race we are told to win, but no one educates us on dealing with the weariness that comes with it.

My art

We get tired of continuous evolution that leaves our

souls drained, but we never work on replenishing our soul. Our entire focus is on staying ahead of others and our own self and that drags us down. How can we counter this when we were never told to focus on our spiritual self? We weren't. At least not until we came to a crossroad in our lives and were unable to decide what road to take. We can only make such a decision when our spiritual self evolves alongside others. My spirituality evolved through my purgatory. It was hell on earth that showed me heaven. It was my wake-up call. Without my hell, I must admit I would have been too blind to see it and perhaps never could have recognized it. I fled my house only to go to another one, where I was meant to be. I learned that these materialistic things are recoverable and easily regenerated.

However, relations and people are irrecoverable. I lost my biological mother, my stepmother, my grandmother, and many other family members and friends. These people I could never resurrect, but I let their death leave a void within me than to carry on with their memories. As inevitable as death is, life taught me to cherish the people who love me more than any other possession because one day they will perish. I learned this through my spiritual awakening.

It was difficult for me to do so as well, as most of the people who had once claimed to be my friends turned their back on me. It is no easy task to find a person who will genuinely care for you. So if you come across such a person, hold them close to you, and offer them your time and love as these traits are priceless. Offer your presence without any expectations. It might seem trivial, but a mere presence can do wonders. If you connect something to it in return, even gratitude, then your soul will be weighed down with expectations. I too had expectations that led me to lead a life in fear. I was afraid of never belonging to anywhere, because I hoped for some sort of consolation. Liberate yourself from wanting something in turn, and offer your smile to those who surround you. Be kind to yourself. Only when I learned to be ok with my nightmares, they stopped and I progressed. With that, you will find yourself inheriting memories that will be your redemption. The smile and laughter I retained from moments of bliss caused me to rise. It was a choice I made.

I was not aware that I could make a choice, that I could navigate my way out until I found God. I discovered that the choices we make are based on nothing but love and fear. These are the only two variants but they both have drastic implications. Choices based on love allow us to transcend beyond the margins and shackles in life. These choices make us decide to prioritize things and values that are vital to humanity instead of anything else. The choices based on fear, however, shackle us.

Our fear is the hindrance that stops us from spreading our wings and soaring in the sky. I wish I could have realized this earlier in life, when I let my time dissipate. Fear blinded me until I could see nothing but pitch darkness. I wish I did not have to go through my hell to learn this. But then I would not have had the opportunity to learn this without all the challenges I have lived through. I could never have recognized my strengths to overcome my fears.

My losses taught me that we die before our physical death. When we succumb to our weakness and fears, we are killing our peace and soul. And what is a person without such? Nothing but a vessel whose body is pumping blood aimlessly. It is our greed to have all the bounties just for ourselves, even when we have more than we can handle. We refrain ourselves from sharing joy and love with those who might need it by surrendering ourselves to the evil within us.

We reduce our circle of life by choosing to lead a life full of fear. There is more to life than this. I learned that life is not about creating abundance for ourselves but abundance for someone else. Our purpose in life is not to have the most expensive car and an extravagant house, but to light up the lives along our path. Freedom for me came from my focus on making a life instead of a living. We already have so little time to do so, yet we drown ourselves in ignorance instead of taking charge and setting things straight. It isn't living to feel stuck in a phase of our lives or frustrated in a job we do not like; it is dying. Still, we stay rooted to our spots, afraid to take a step in another direction. Afraid of taking chances and afraid of anticipation, so much so that we willingly kill ourselves. Dying itself is so much easier than anything else we encounter in this life.

We just never take a chance and step out of our comfort zone. We fear failure more than death, to the point that we overlook on making the most of the time we are given to spend on this earth. Now, I don't quite remember all the things I did for myself, but I can recall the things I did for others because of the magnitude of their smiles.

Their eyes, gleaming with unspoken emotions, became souvenirs for me to preserve. What I do for others is more likely to fulfill my soul than materialistic things. The comfort that resonates from these smiles is what lets me know that my presence was appreciated. I was loved. Love is the very substance of life. Life without love is incomplete. Life without love makes us feel weak and is tasteless. Love is something that can never be bought or taken by force, but is earned with our efforts and time.

Hand molds of my hospice patient's hand with her loved one's hand. I love creating these for families I work with in hospice. I spend my weekends in my studio carving and preparing them.

Only we limit ourselves from splurging on love. We create a fear-based reality that foregoes love. We fog up our own vision, which leads us to stumble and fall. Instead of getting up, for far too long I let myself down. I lived a life where fear-based love marginalized my existence. I was too afraid to rely on someone, and that eventually led me to drive people away. The fear of rejection kept me from the thought of not telling someone how I felt. I was so desperate just to be part of a group that I overlooked how I was surrounding myself with people who perceived me as a means of entertainment. It was my fear that led me to stay amidst a crowd of familiar faces, but I could never connect with them.

We live a life in fear more than love. Fear, however, does not end at the lack of belongingness. It is vast. It goes beyond not having enough or not being enough. It imprisons us into not living our best lives. It is a black hole in which we fall endlessly, a bolt on the lock that limits our freedom and happiness. On the other hand, love is limitless. Love creates freedom and the ability to fully exist in the moment. It breaks our imaginary chains and allows us to count all our blessings instead of dwelling on sadness.

We continue to create our life based on the choices we make and the motives behind our actions. It is our perception that dictates our experiences. From previously pitying myself, I changed my perception of myself and saw myself as a survivor. My perception of events dictates my reality. If I see myself as a victim, then everything around me will justify it. On the contrary, a survivor sees things that help us push forward. I learned how to see the grass as green everywhere I went instead of feeling like I had left something behind. Even in the death of my family members, as hard as it was, I saw how their journey was only meant to last until a certain age.

From there, they would want me to continue walking. I changed my perception of this, and it enabled me to stand up and move on while holding onto the memories of love. From my life, I saw that I was never alone. That many like me were suffering in silence when we did not have to. From my misfortune, I counted the priceless possessions that helped me turn the sail of my life around. Where I was once heading blindly toward a hurricane, thinking my life was pointless, I now saw the ropes that were at my disposal. I let go of my fear that was weighing my boat down. This allowed me to maneuver the ropes accordingly, and I led myself away from my doom. When I was making my way successfully toward the shore, I realized I could help those on crashing boats, and those drowning. I wish to help all the stranded and lost by sharing my fears and my life with you. I dedicate this book to all of you. You, who have grieved in silence for fear of being judged. You who have suppressed your sobs just so you don't disrupt the sleep of another. You, who have grieved alone as others ran from you the moment you had nothing to offer. You, who watched your heartbreak while you wept in silence and blamed yourself. You who wanted to give up, yet mustered the courage to sit wherever you are and read these words. You, the imperfect, the fallen ones with no one to pick you up.

We all fall frequently in life. Rise. You are a survivor. You are stronger than you think. You can pick your own burden and put back your pieces together. You have not lost, but won a battle by choosing to be here. You are a beautiful creation that is one of a kind. Be true to yourself. Life is not about perfection. Look beyond the mirage of a new horizon, and you will find you were never lost. Do not seek a home in a concrete building, but within the smiles of those around you. Look around you, and you will know that you are home. Do not define your life with all the wealth you have acquired, but measure your deeds by their humility and compassion. Stumble but do not falter from your own shadow. Life is about getting up when we fall. It is about embracing ourselves no matter what imperfections we have. Remember, no one is perfect and we all have limited time. We all have one life. Make the most of it. Leave behind memories to be cherished. Leave behind footprints of love to guide others to follow, until they are able to direct themselves in life. In turn, become better and stronger together. Be courageous. Let these words be your Holy Grail.

"Our greatest glory is not in never falling, but in rising every time we fall."

-Confucius

My father and I

LEJLA BECIROVIC

Made in the
USA
Lexington, KY